UNBEATABLE MIND

DEVELOP MENTAL TOUGHNESS AND IMPROVE SOCIAL SKILLS TO ACHIEVE ANYTHING YOU WANT IN LIFE

SKYLER MCCARTY

© Copyright 2019 by Skyler McCarty

All rights reserved. No part of this publication may be reproduced, distributed, or transmitted in any form or by any means, including photocopying, recording, or other electronic or mechanical methods, without the prior written permission of the publisher, except in the case of brief quotations embodied in critical reviews and certain other noncommercial uses permitted by copyright law.

The following book is reproduced below with the goal of providing information that is as accurate and reliable as possible. Regardless, purchasing this book can be seen as consent to the fact that both the publisher and the author of this book are in no way experts on the topics discussed within and that any recommendations or suggestions that are made herein are for entertainment purposes only. Professionals should be consulted as needed prior to undertaking any of the action endorsed herein.

The information in the following pages is broadly considered to be a truthful and accurate account of facts and as such any inattention, use or misuse of the information in question by the reader will render any resulting actions solely under their purview. There are no scenarios in which the publisher or the original author of this work can be in any fashion deemed liable for any hardship or damages that may befall them after undertaking information described herein.

Additionally, the information in the following pages is intended only for informational purposes and should thus be thought of as universal. As befitting its nature, it is presented without assurance regarding its prolonged validity or interim quality. Trademarks that are mentioned are done without written consent and can in no way be considered an endorsement from the trademark holder.

CONTENTS

1. MENTAL TOUGHNESS

PART ONE
Introduction 5
1. Taking Back Control of Your Life 13
2. Controlling Your Emotions 23

PART TWO
3. Setting Your Long-Term and Short-Term Goals ... 35
4. Uncovering Your Burning Desire to Win ... 47
5. Developing a Warrior Mindset, Self-Discipline, and Unbreakable Habits ... 55

PART THREE
6. Stepping out of Your Comfort Zone 67
7. Dealing with Failures and Becoming More Resilient ... 75

PART FOUR
8. The Importance of Self-Confidence and Self-Belief ... 85
9. Visualization, Positive Thinking, Journaling, & Meditation ... 95

Conclusion 105

2. OVERCOMING SOCIAL ANXIETY

Introduction 109

PART ONE
UNDERSTANDING SOCIAL ANXIETY
1. What is Social Anxiety? 115
2. The Symptoms of Social Anxiety 119
3. Causes of Social Anxiety 123
4. Understanding What Goes On In Your Brain 129

PART TWO
THE DEEP UNDERLYING PROBLEM
5. Your Limiting Beliefs 135
6. Learn to Accept Yourself 141
7. Increase Self-Confidence and Self-Esteem to Beat Social Anxiety 147

PART THREE
4 STEPS TO OVERCOME SOCIAL ANXIETY
8. Change the stories you tell yourself 157
9. Stop Being Overly Self-Conscious 169
10. Learn to Control Your Breathing 173
11. Put Yourself Out There 177

PART FOUR
LIFESTYLE CHANGES TO REDUCE ANXIETY
12. Diet & Exercises 187
13. Mindfulness 193

PART FIVE
30-DAY CHALLENGE TO OVERCOME SOCIAL ANXIETY
14. Before the Challenge 199

15. The 30-Day Challenge	203
Conclusion	211

3. COMMUNICATION IN MARRIAGE

Introduction	217
1. The Truth about Happy Marriages	223
2. The Communication Differences between Men and Women	237
3. Common Problems and the Best Ways to Handle Them	247
4. Understanding and Changing What's Wrong	261
5. Communication Skills Mastery	279
6. Proven Actions to Improve Your Relationship	291
Conclusion	303
Author's Note	307
About the Author	309

1. MENTAL TOUGHNESS

HOW TO DEVELOP WARRIOR MINDSET, SELF-DISCIPLINE, AND UNBREAKABLE HABITS TO ACHIEVE MASSIVE SUCCESS AND HAPPINESS

PART ONE

CONTROL

INTRODUCTION

Have you ever wondered why some people are naturally more successful than others? Maybe you have always envied your friend down the street for their ease of talking to others and getting ahead in life. Does it frustrate you knowing that you cannot achieve the same success?

Perhaps you have considered the fact that something about this person sets them apart. They make more money than you, they have more friends, they are better at managing their time, being parents, just about everything. All you know is, you don't have whatever it is they possess that makes them leap and bound ahead of you.

The answer of 'why' may have eluded you for quite some time. In your search for more clarity and a magic bullet to make all of your dreams come true, you may have figured out that basic skills like intelligence and talent aren't all that is required for success. After all, many talented people have wasted their gifts by not continuing to grow and enhance their skills. The answer could be mental toughness.

It could be that this person and others around you, simply have more sheer willpower to accomplish their goals than you do. They are able to identify and focus on what is important, and set out to complete tasks and reach new levels of success, both monetarily and socially.

The good news is, it is entirely possible to work on the underlying skill of mental toughness to get closer to reaching your goals. This book is dedicated to the process of identifying your mental strengths and weaknesses and finding ways to play into your strengths while boosting your areas of weakness.

From this point forward, consider working your brain as if you would work your body. You do sit-ups and planks to strengthen your core muscles, and so too should you practice certain exercises to enhance and maintain your mental toughness. As you know, muscle growth does not happen overnight. It takes a strong consistency of workouts to see any difference, and developing mental toughness is no different. Developing a good pattern of self-discipline, emotional intelligence, motivation, and persistence is key to creating the life you have always dreamed for yourself.

What is Mental Toughness?

Mental toughness is the ability of a person to power through tough times with the same strength and vigor they could carry when things are going right. In the case of the entrepreneur, it is the ability to promote your business and do all of the necessary things to run the business even when you are struggling. It is so easy to succumb to negative thoughts and the desire to quit. Having the ability to walk through the fire instead of finding a way around is what sets you apart from your peers and advances you in life.

You must choose your path and maintain your focus despite distraction to meet your goals. Even the perception of 'having it good' and tasting a small amount of success can derail us. We can't slack off and work less just because we have reached a small level of success. You worked hard to get there and you need to continue working hard to maintain your status and advance it.

The Four C's of Mental Toughness

Let us now take a look at the Four C's of Mental Toughness. The model was based on an existing model of Hardiness as described by Kobassa (1979), who proposed three components of control, challenge, and commitment. Clough later identified a fourth component of mental toughness — confidence.

Control

The idea of having control over your life can certainly put you ahead of the curve. You will feel like you have the power over your situation, able to make your own money, solve your own problems and do what you want. Control is also about emotions, and the ability to remain even-keeled when things are going wrong. For example, the measure of a good leader is their level of calm under pressure.

Being able to power through any situation with the same demeanor shows other that you are in control, and even settles people down. When people feel that their leader, president or CEO, is not worried about a situation, it gives the illusion of safety and security, two things that can maintain normalcy even in the face of enormous pressure. To be clear, it is not always possible to avoid your emotions, but you can control how you react to any given situation, and that takes a great deal of mental toughness.

Commitment

Think about your life or that of someone close to you. Does it ever seem like you just can't stick with anything? Maybe you tried going to college but was not struck by any particular subject. You switched majors every semester, and now have a degree that hangs on the wall, and yet has no use in your current career choice. If this sounds oddly specific, it is because I have had some experience in this area.

Commitment is all about finding something you want to do and sticking with it. When it comes to careers, it can be difficult to know if you are doing the right thing, and sometimes you won't be. The difference is, you need to do your best to ring each and every possible experience out of your failed career choice before you go.

Think about your career in terms of a straight line. Have you made linear steps that bring you closer to your goal? Did you finish school, find a job in your field and climb the ladder to success? Or, did you waiver on your choice, finish school behind schedule, find a job outside your field, then return? The first scenario could be visualized by a straight line, while the second is a zigzag. Straighten that line out and find that it is twice the length because it took you twice as long. Meanwhile, you could have advanced further in your career faster by setting goals and remaining focused on them through completion.

Challenge

No successful person ever advanced themselves by playing it safe. Success in life is all about adapting and being resourceful. Trying and learning new things is at the heart of that. We cannot grow and advance our skills if we sit in the same office, doing the same unchallenging work we have done for years on end. Once you find yourself getting bored or having mastered something, it is time to build on it.

Think about your first job. Did you know everything there was to know about selling ice cream cones? Probably not. Your first day, your manager probably showed you how to scoop the ice cream while they rang out the sales. When you got comfortable scooping, they showed you how to run the register. You took things one step at a time. You must be your own manager and set small, manageable goals for yourself, and do your best to reach them.

Confidence

When you know in your heart that you know what you're doing and you are on the right path for you, confidence blooms. This takes a bit of time and soul-searching, but once you are confident with your focus, it will become much easier to keep it. We must have confidence in everything that we do in order to be successful. Good self-confidence gives us the power to persuade others to help us. Believing that achieving your goals is the first step in getting there. No self-help was ever written about the power of negative self-talk, so instead, focus on being positive about yourself, your path and your choices and the rest will soon fall into place.

If you have connected on some level with any of the concepts I have talked about in this introduction, this book may just be for you. We can all make improvements to our mental toughness, and doing so can propel us forward in all aspects of our lives. If you are like me and have often felt that you are spinning your wheels trying to find success, take the ideas in this book to heart. You can certainly attain the lofty goals you have always imagined for yourself, but it takes focus and mental toughness. You need to create a plan with small goals to lift you to that level you have desired. The first rung on that ladder is developing your mental toughness.

Before you begin, I recommend taking a short test, called the MTQ48. This test was developed by Professor Peter Clough of Manchester Metropolitan University, Dr Keith Earle, Senior Lecturer, at the University of Hull and Doug Strycharczyk, Managing Director of AQR.

Its purpose is to quantitatively measure mental toughness by looking at overall character, grit during tough situations, and emotional control.

The results of this test can help you determine your mental strengths and weaknesses and provide a starting point for your journey to mental toughness. The MTQ48 test can be found online through a number of resources.

I hope you enjoy the content of this book. Good luck!

ONE

TAKING BACK CONTROL OF YOUR LIFE

> *Only you can control your future.*
>
> DR. SEUSS

THE VERY FIRST thing that you need to realize is that you, and you alone, are responsible for how your life plays out. The thoughts, decisions, and actions that you make are what drives your life. No longer can you float through life waiting for something to happen for you. We also can't expect to rely on others either.

This last sentence really hits home for me. There was a time in my life where I was in love so deeply that I would want to spend every moment possible with my spouse. We just loved being together and I would often forgo other plans, including doing school work and studying, just to hang out. Long term, this has had a major effect on my life. The term co-dependency comes to mind, as I placed every ounce of my self-worth and happiness in this one person. I sabotaged my own success in most areas of my life to tend to just one relationship.

On a happy note, I am still with said spouse, but I have drastically changed the way I look at our relationship. I no longer wait to see what he is doing after work before making my own plans. I was never forced by this person to comply with certain expectations, I did that all by myself. These days, my happiness is enhanced by the relationship but is not defined by it. I am able to accomplish my own goals with the support I need, but I am earning my degree and mapping out my own successes as an individual.

I would encourage you to look at your situation. Whether you are in a relationship or not, there is likely someone or something that is holding you back.

You may have even said, *"If only I could be in a relationship, I would be happy. If I had a bigger house, I would be happy. If so and so would quit this job so I could move up, I would be happy."*

Whatever the case may be, it does not matter. Making these statements, even thinking them, is a scapegoat for doing the real work.

Our lives are in our hands. If we work hard and make the right connections at work, we can move up without so and so quitting. Being in a relationship may make you miserable as well, so find other things that make you happy. On another note, bigger houses mean bigger headaches, not happiness.

Stop making excuses and placing blame for your situation on others. You are in control and it is high time you take responsibility for your own actions. Stop playing the victim.

Victimizing yourself can be a very hard habit to break. To help get you started, I challenge you to go a whole week without complaining. After all, complaining is really blaming. No more blabbing about how bad traffic was when you should have left earlier. Don't complain that a co-worker isn't pulling their weight. Don't wish things were different, and definitely, avoid "if only" statements.

Instead, reroute your thinking to try and find a simple solution to whatever problem you are having. Complaining never actually solves a problem. Straightening up your attitude will not only improve your overall attitude and outlook on your situation, others, including your employer, will take notice.

What you 'want' vs getting what you want

Saying you want something and actually getting it are two different things. Anyone can say they want a big house on the beach and a fancy car, but only those with mental toughness will connect the dots between "I want" and "I have". You may want something, but don't want to put in the hard work to get (and deserve) it. The value of your life and the things in it are a reflection of your hard work. There is no other way unless you get lucky and win the lottery. Seeing as that is highly unlikely, put those eggs in your own basket, invest in yourself and make your success that way.

To get what you want, first, you need to visualize it. Perhaps you are really shallow and only care about the fancy house and the car. Honestly, that will be a sad life once you get there. Or maybe you see the fancy house and car, with a boatload of family and friends around to share it with you. Really think about what it is that you want. Is it the tangible things? Or is it the security of having a house to live in, a reliable car and a family to love?

Often times, the things we imagine having are only the physical manifestation of our emotional needs. While tangible things are nice, cut through the clouds to see what is really important. The life you carve out for yourself is likely to include the same detail, but you can certainly still fulfill those emotional needs without so much stuff.

Be like Maya Angelou and make your life happen. Don't sit around waiting for the right time, or the right person to come along to 'begin' your life. It is already happening. The first step is to get in control of our thoughts and emotions. We need to fully understand the emotions that drive our lives in order to make changes and determine a path that will best suit us.

For example, perhaps you have stayed at a certain career because you feel taking a pay cut to do what you really want to is not realistic. In turn, you remain stressed and a bit depressed about your situation, emotions that get squashed for the sake of convenience. Take the time to sort through those thoughts and emotions and give them the attention they need. Emotions are the body's way of telling us that something is wrong. Ignoring them is like ignoring the warning signs of a heart attack.

Taking a chance and reworking your focus onto something you truly love will certainly bring you success. Anytime you feel passionate about something, it makes it much easier to stay motivated about reaching the next milestone.

What about the fear of failure?

Self-doubt is a real buzzkill. We have all had feelings of inadequacy at one time or another, and it will likely rear its ugly head sometime in the future. This is where the idea of self-confidence comes in. Instead of getting caught up in the "What if I fail" scenario, change your thinking to, "What if I fly". Don't let your doubts consume you and change your goals.

Fear of failure is a common problem felt by everyone. The idea that you may not be able to accomplish your goals because of your shortcomings is a good reason not to try. Facing the fact that you may not have the skills necessary is much scarier than never having tried at all. Not trying suggests that you could have done well if you had tried, but not a complete failure.

Honestly, trying and going for gold is much braver than not having tried at all. Most people who have tried and failed feel much more self-confidence as they have pushed past their fears, which is a goal in itself. Yes, they may have failed to reach their objective entirely, but many other positive things may have happened on the way.

Maybe you don't think of fear of failure, or atychiphobia, as something that is holding you back. Or perhaps you simply can't recognize the signs. Procrastinating can often be associated with fear of failure. You put off starting or finishing something often out of fear of the unknown. It is common to be anxious about completing things you have never done before or getting overwhelmed by the workload in front of you. Think about those term papers you had to write in school. A twenty-page paper seemed like an insurmountable task.

In order to help build our mental toughness, it is important to get past the procrastination hump and just get started. Just do the next thing. No matter how small, do one thing today that is going to get you closer to your goal. Use this motivational technique to get you through a pile of paperwork. Pick up the next piece, do what needs to be done and file it away. Handle each piece with attention only on that, and those overwhelming feelings melt away.

Fear of failure can also manifest itself with physical symptoms, like an upset stomach before a presentation. You may also avoid telling people about your plans to complete something so that if things don't work out, nobody has to know. You may say things like, "I think I can get this done on time", or "I might be able to make it", giving you an out if you fail to live up to your word.

Make Time for Self-Care

The only real way to get in touch with our emotional needs and lift ourselves out of the victim mentality is to take care of ourselves first. We are often driven to satisfy the needs of others, getting to work early, staying late, running errands, and doing favors for friends and family. While this is all necessary in life, we need to stop short and make sure we are giving ourselves the same attention.

Our mental health is usually the first casualty. Make sure to set aside time for your own well-being each and every day. Change your habits to include things like meditation, proper sleep, exercise and healthy eating. Nourishing your body and mind will pay you back in spades, and make you a streamlined machine that is ready to focus on the next big task, instead of just slugging through life.

Take time to really think about what you want, and re-evaluate your goals on the regular. Staying focused on a task, like starting your own business, takes a great deal of checking in. Write lists of things to do, check in on your progress, and set new objectives for yourself. Just remember to keep your ultimate goal in mind.

The Takeaway

- You, and you only, are responsible for the outcomes of your life.
- Stop blaming others for things that are (or aren't) happening in your life.
- Start with a 7-day 'no complaining' challenge. Instead of complaining, take a look at possible solutions to your problems.

- Recognize signs of fear of failure, like procrastination and downplaying your goals.
- Make time to take care of yourself, mind, body and spirit.

TWO
CONTROLLING YOUR EMOTIONS

> *You cannot always control what goes on outside. But you can always control what goes on inside.*
>
> WAYNE DYER

GET YOUR EMOTIONS UNDER CONTROL. Stop listening to them so much and think logically instead. Well, that is all easier said than done. Our emotions exist as the body's way of telling us something isn't quite right.

When you feel uncomfortable in a situation where you are physically in danger or are mentally confronted, your body sends signals of anger, sadness, and discontent, all in an attempt to move you out of that space. Emotions are meant to move you, physically and emotionally, out of harm's way.

That being said, it is vitally important to consider your emotions, but control your corresponding actions in their response. Emotional stability is a key factor to mental toughness. When you allow your emotions to run your life exclusively, you are more likely to get off track with your goals. It will be very difficult to stay focused on what needs to be done when your emotions, more often than not, fear, are pulling you in different directions.

In order to overcome the fears and anxieties that prevent us from succeeding, we need to develop our emotional intelligence. While working in the same facets of life, emotional intelligence and mental toughness are a little bit different.

Emotional intelligence is the ability to understand what you are feeling, why you are feeling it, and rationally dealing with it.

For example, an unfair situation at work may make you feel angry. Your boss has given a coveted project to a co-worker, and you are upset that you didn't get it. We can already determine that you are upset, but the cause is likely deeper set than this project. Thinking further, you realize that it is your feelings of insecurity and low self-worth that make you feel upset. The situation causes you to call your skills and abilities into question.

Now that you are aware of why you feel this way, you can react accordingly. First, sit with that feeling, aware that it exists. Feeling down in the dumps can be a strong motivator for change, should it be necessary. Next, bring yourself back up. You have shown your capabilities time and time again. Besides, you are already elbow-deep in another project. There is no way you could handle both right now. Maybe your boss made the right call.

Being able to do this very quickly and avoiding the sometimes-unavoidable overreaction is critical. How many times have you jumped to conclusions, allowed your emotions to get away from you, and said something you didn't really mean? Regret usually follows as you have time to think things through.

Emotional intelligence comes with time and practice. Get into the habit of checking in with your emotions often, at least a couple of times per day when you are feeling pretty normal, and even more when you start feeling anxious, upset or panicked. Take the time to rationally think the emotions through before carrying on with your day. Over time you will begin to recognize patterns in your thinking and will be able to stop that downward spiral of negativity in its tracks.

Keeping a journal and jotting down a few notes as you are doing it helps clear out those emotions. They are also useful for reflection further down the line. Often reading an entry back makes you realize how unrealistic and emotional you were being, aiding in the process of making you more stable should the situation arise again.

Franklin D. Roosevelt has been quoted saying "There is nothing to fear but fear itself". This quote has more weight than you may realize. The common fear of failure or irrational things that hold you back is the reason we fail. The difference between someone who succeeds and someone who doesn't is their ability to overcome this emotion, and push through despite it. It is not that successful people do not have obstacles to overcome, it is that they have the tenacity to fight past the fear for the sake of progress.

How to overcome your greatest enemy – Fear

Overcoming fear is a constant and necessary process. If you are truly pushing forward toward your goals, you are likely facing a multitude of fears each and every day. For example, if your goal is to become a doctor, you are facing difficult classes and challenges all the time. You are learning new things. You are competing for rank with classmates, juggling classes, and a part-time job. If you are already at this phase, your goals are in motion. But what about overcoming the fear of getting started?

Too many people stop their success before it even has a chance to get started. It is much easier to talk yourself out of doing the hard work than it is to do it. Maintaining your current life is easy, because you are already doing it. Making changes and moving forward is difficult, and if you are not willing to overcome the fear of change, fear of failure, then you will always be stuck.

To get past this, use daily affirmations. You are good enough, and you are worthy of the success that you seek. You are ultimately in charge of how your life plays out, so it is solely up to you to make sure you find success. Say it out loud. Every day. Yes, your mind will come up with excuses to calm you back down. Argue with yourself, push those doubtful thoughts to the back of your mind. This will be an ongoing process, but over time, it will become easier to keep control of these negative thoughts.

There are lots of little things you can do to boost your self-confidence each and every day. First, define your goals. Saying you want to have a big house and fancy cars is not a goal. It is the result of reaching your goal. You cannot simply have those things, you need to work for them. So, your goal should be something you can actually do, like starting a business or furthering your current career.

Going after that goal is like trying to go somewhere you have never been without a map. Sure, you might get lucky and pick the right set of roads to get to your destination, but why not look at the map? At least you will know you are headed in the right direction. With any goal, it is important to make a map of how you plan to get there. This doesn't have to be complicated.

For example, becoming a medical doctor would be a long process. Your map may see you passing undergrad classes, applying to medical school, interning, and passing the tests. The minute details can get overwhelming so for right now, just hit the big ones. As you go, think ahead regularly in preparation for the next step. For example, start working on your med school applications well in advance of the deadlines to show yourself off properly.

What about stress?

How do we manage stress? Like fear, stress is the body's response to unfavorable conditions. Our heart rates increase, our hands get sweaty, and we can easily become overwhelmed. This could be in acute response to a big presentation at work, or chronic in response to a tough living situation. Whatever the case may be, the stress is unlikely to go away unless the stimulus does. Stress is usually maintained by a hectic, busy schedule and lots of things to do. Unfortunately, going after success usually puts us right in the middle of this.

To counteract stress, we must do a few different things. First, we must conquer whatever acute fears we have, like getting anxious before the presentation. Positive self-talk will calm you down and being well prepared will boost your confidence. Imagine giving a talk on a topic you know nothing about. People will ask questions that you can't answer. It likely won't be very successful. On the other hand, talking about something that you have researched backward and forward will give you the confidence to answer every question and breeze through the material effortlessly. Which would have you less stressed?

Stress will occur; there is no alternative. We need to learn to manage our stress properly to keep functioning well. Imagine that your stress is water in a steam kettle. As the pot warms, the water molecules get restless, bouncing about the kettle. As more and more molecules turn to steam, the pressure builds as all the molecules want to do is get out. Eventually, the kettle whistles, as the steam rushes out.

Now think about this in relation to your life. Being

late for work, having a bad meeting, missing the bus home, having to put dinner on the table for your family, and everything that happens in between cause the heat beneath the kettle to increase. You need to actively let off that steam throughout the day to avoid blowing up.

How do you make time for stress relief activities when your schedule causes you stress? Start building at set times, like appointments, for these things. Set aside fifteen minutes a few times per day to take a break. This time can be used for meditation, yoga, catching a few winks, and organizing your day. This short period of time could be all you need to refocus your brain, calm your nerves and get ready to finish tackling your day.

Sleep is a huge contributor to stress as well. Sleeping well and long enough re-energizes your brain and resets it to handle the pressures of the following day. Feeling well rested and recharged sets the tone for the rest of the day. Get to sleep early and set aside electronics at least an hour before bed. Take this time to read for pleasure, journal, or meditate.

Using preventive measures to counteract stress is one thing, but what do we do about very stressful, acute situations? You may not be able to step away to think, so how can you stay calm in the midst of a high-pressure situation? This will inevitably happen, and let's use our big presentation example to highlight this.

Maybe you prepared the best you could, but your audience is really grilling you about the details. Even with your extensive knowledge of the subject, these people are out to get you, nit-picking everything.

Your goal here is to stay calm and deflect. Previous experience has shown that honesty is the best way out of a situation like this. Owning up to a problem with your theory or product looks much better than trying to defend it and backing yourself into a corner. Take deep breaths and take a couple of seconds to contemplate your answer before carrying on. Remember that even important meetings have do-overs. Most business is done outside of the conference room anyway. Keep yourself from thinking that this is your last chance at success, because it probably isn't, and the stress associated with it does more harm than good.

The Takeaway

- Improving emotional intelligence helps you cope with emotions and keep them from halting your success.
- You need to overcome and conquer fears to truly succeed. No more shying away from them, face them head-on.

- Work on stress-reducing techniques by building time for them into your day.
- Stay calm under stress by owning up to your problems.

PART TWO

COMMITMENT

THREE
SETTING YOUR LONG-TERM AND SHORT-TERM GOALS

> *First say to yourself what you would be; and then do what you have to do.*
>
> EPICTETUS

Remember that without a clear goal and a roadmap to get there, we will get lost. It is not good enough to daydream about your successes, you must get there. However, there is a major difference between the dream and the reality.

Truly successful people have had the ability to put concrete steps in-between these things in order to realize their ultimate goals.

Let's start with the long-term plan. First, you must know what it is you want to achieve. Pinpointing what this is can be the hardest part for some people. As I said before, having a big house and fancy cars is not the dream, it is a result of it. You need to dig a little deeper to find out what it is that gets you there.

Perhaps you aren't influenced much by wealth. Instead, you see yourself as a different person. Maybe your current state is one of dissatisfaction with your appearance, your health, and your abilities to get out in the world. You see yourself out walking your dogs, running marathons and cooking healthy meals for your family. For many, this is a lofty goal, and they often remain unhealthy because they cannot figure out how to connect the dots.

Whatever your dream may be, thinking about how to get it all at once is very overwhelming. Therefore, it is necessary to set smaller, more attainable short-term goals. This is the idea of successive approximation. These goals should be geared toward pushing you in the right direction in order to someday reach your ultimate goal. For example, if better health and ideal weight is your overall goal, a smaller set of goals would be:

- Take a healthy cooking class to build up your cooking skills
- Commit to exercising 5 days a week
- Meeting with a nutritionist to set yourself up for success.

With any goal, making lifestyle changes leads to success. Committing to losing fifty pounds is a big step which will fail if you are not setting smaller goals for yourself.

The same goes with career goals. Perhaps you want to become the top-grossing salesperson at your company. You do not simply do that. Instead, making smaller goals and building new habits will help you do this. Commit to making a minimum set of number of phone calls per day, set a schedule for meeting with new clients, and work on leadership development. Plan to attend at least one marketing event per month. Whatever your long-term goal is, set yourself up for success by challenging yourself to do smaller, less scary things every day. Eventually, you will find yourself poised to reach your ultimate goal.

For successive approximation to be successful, it must be done at the beginning, and at any turn in the road to success. For example, if reaching a healthy weight is your ultimate goal, your first step after deciding that you will take action is creating your plan. Your smaller goals could be losing five pounds, then ten, then twenty. Each goal should be met with a set of bullet points for how you plan to accomplish it. Each step should also have an evaluation and redevelopment stage.

Along the way, you need to evaluate whether or

not the actions you are taking are bringing you success. It is at this point that you need to decide whether to give it more time or change your plan. Maybe getting to the gym 5 days a week isn't working with your schedule, therefore it is not effective. Reworking the plan to include 2 gym days and 3 more days of workouts at home could be more effective. Just make sure not to downgrade your goal to simplify things. Making changes is hard, and it does take time to adjust to a new routine.

Let's delve a little bit more into our goal setting techniques to set up some concrete goals. We will use the SMART method as we work.

Using a concrete set of steps like SMART to set concrete goals just seems right. The good news is, it has been proven highly effective. SMART is an acronym for '**specific, measurable, attainable, realistic and timely**' goals. A goal that fits all of these definitions is more likely to be achieved than lofty, unrealistic ones.

Specific

Pick a tangible goal, like becoming a doctor, rather than something vague, like earning fame and fortune. How will you do this? Use the question words, "who, what, when, where, why and how" to help specify your goal. Pay careful attention to the "why" and "how". Do you have a good reason for wanting to pursue something? Do you have a true passion for it or is wealth a big contributing factor? Also, "how" you plan to do something is vital.

Measurable

How will you know when you have achieved this goal? Achieving an ideal fitness level is great, but what are your markers for success? Will you reach a goal weight? Will you be able to run a marathon? With your career, will you call success being the CEO of your company? Making a specific amount of money?

Attainable

Saying your goal is to lose fifty pounds by next Friday is downright impossible. The trademark of any good goal is to be reasonable and attainable. Don't set your sights on an impossible deadline. All it will do is make you lose confidence in yourself, and you will be primed to let yourself down. There are also certain goals that you simply can't reach. For example, you may reach a point where you decide that being the CEO of your company isn't realistic. The current CEO isn't going anywhere, and your position just below CEO is hitting the mark, besides the title. It is important to be specific, but flexible so attainability is still intact.

Realistic

If you can't sing, pursuing a music career isn't realistic. The key terms here are "willing" and "able". You must have the passion and motivation to be a musician, but if you are not able to sing, the goal is unrealistic. This part isn't meant to crush your dreams, but it is important to consider the possible pitfalls of your goals. Go ahead and dream big but be honest with yourself. Should you continue to seek a record deal, or should you make alterations to your goal to make it more tangible. Maybe you could start a record company instead. Facilitating the process for others can be just as rewarding.

Timely

People are naturally impatient, so make sure your goals can be reached in a relatively short period of time. Your short-term goals should be built to give yourself some instant gratification to keep you motivated. For example, with weight loss, making a meeting with a nutritionist a goal is easily attainable, and can be done relatively quickly. Crossing that off your list and moving on to something else (like following through with your new meal plan) will feel good and set you up for success.

Putting a timeframe on things creates the sense of urgency you need to carry through as well. If you want to lose fifty pounds, it can reasonably be done over the course of a year, or you could drag it out for five years. If you feel a little more pressure, it will likely drive you to complete your small goals much faster to avoid feeling as though you have failed.

Use the exercise below to help put a good framework behind setting your goal. Whether you are just contemplating beginning a new venture, or are smack dab in the middle, taking some time to evaluate where you are and plan your next steps is always helpful. I would recommend physically writing down your progress.

Keep the document somewhere where you can look at it again. Remember that assessing and re-evaluating your goals is part of the process.

SMART Goal Setting Exercise

Specific:

What is your goal?
_____

When do you plan to complete it?
_____

Why do you want to do it?
_____

Where will this be done?
_____

Who will be involved with this venture?
_____

How do you plan to do this?
_____

How will you know when you have reached this goal? List at least 2 measures of success.

_____

_____

Attainable:

List three smaller goals that need to be reached in order to reach your ultimate goal.

_____

_____

_____

Realistic:

Are you willing to accomplish this goal or are outside people/factors affecting your decisions?

_____

Are you able (physically, mentally, emotionally ready) to accomplish this goal?

_____

Timely:

What is your timeline for completion?

_____

Now and then, take a look at the first page where you have set the specifics of your goal. Next, it is time to determine whether you are meeting these goals, and where adjustments need to be made. Be honest and realistic. These are your goals and it is important to really think about where you are and how to continue making your success.

Is your goal still realistic or have circumstances changed?
_____
Are you on track to meet your deadline?
_____
What strategies for success are working well?
_____
What strategies are not working well?
_____

The Takeaway

- Goals should be specific, measurable, attainable, realistic, and timely.
- Use successive approximation to set small

goals that step you up to your ultimate ones.
- Being honest and realistic about your progress is the best way to determine your success. Inflating the truth does not help motivate you!

FOUR
UNCOVERING YOUR BURNING DESIRE TO WIN

> *The desire to win is born in most of us. The will to win is a matter of training. The manner of winning is a matter of honor.*
>
> MARGARET THATCHER

THERE IS no doubt that ultimate success has a lot to do with your passion and desire for it. The problem is, desire can often be fleeting, leaving you motivated to make major changes in your life one day, but not the next. What can you do to increase your motivation to keep moving towards your goals?

First, we need to understand the difference between intrinsic and extrinsic motivation. Simply put, intrinsic motivation is motivation that comes from inside you. It is the desire to do things simply out of the sheer want to do them. For example, if you truly like running as a hobby, you will be motivated to do it. Intrinsic motivation does not require a reward outside of completing an activity, the task itself brings joy and satisfaction.

Building your goals and dreams around your intrinsic motivations is a great idea. If there are things that take a little effort to get going, you should definitely be including them in your regular routine. For example, if you enjoy writing stories and researching new topics, writing books or starting a blog could be a natural extension of those hobbies and skills. Writing skills can be helpful to just about any realm of expertise, it would just be a matter of learning how to incorporate it.

Extrinsic motivation is motivation that comes from outside yourself. You can be driven by the promise of a raise at work, earning a new outfit once you lose five pounds or any other reward for getting something done. Sure, this may mean you are doing some things for less than virtuous reasons, but things are getting done just the same.

At this point in time, you need to evaluate what you are doing throughout your day. Is it mostly driven by intrinsic or extrinsic motivation? Are you working for the Friday paycheck, or do you intrinsically enjoy what you are doing? Keep in mind that work is work, and the idea that 'doing something you love means never working a day in your life', isn't feasible.

You can be drawn to a certain field intrinsically, but there will still be things to do in between majorly exciting projects. Keeping your business afloat, answering emails and doing other boring tasks are just part of life. It is the extrinsic motivation, like rewarding yourself after a tough day that pushes you through. You need to understand that the less-than-desirable activities are necessary to reach your ultimate goals. You need both intrinsic and extrinsic motivation to lead a well-balanced life.

Now, look at your life. Are you living up to your full potential through mostly intrinsic motivation, or are you being pushed along by the perceived rewards of your extrinsic rewards? As you think about the life you have always dreamed of living, think about how this is a powerful intrinsic reward, and how much more you could be succeeding if you included more things that strike this chord more often.

Growing your Desire

> *"The starting point of all achievement is desire. Keep this constantly in mind. Weak*

desire brings weak results, just as a small fire makes a small amount of heat."

NAPOLEON HILL

Napoleon Hill was an interesting character. Back in 1937, he published a book called, *Think and Grow Rich*. The book outlined his thirteen tips for success and building wealth, a culmination of what he learned during his time working with Andrew Carnegie, one of the richest men during that period.

Many of the points made in this book are still true today. First, you must have a clear distinction of your desire. Just like the specificity in the SMART training, your desire must be specific enough to write it down. Only with this clarity can it possibly come true. Napoleon Hill also understood that with any gain there must be a corresponding sacrifice. What are you willing to trade about your current life to gain what you ultimately desire? This does not mean giving up your first born, but cutting way back on TV time is a nice trade for a greater good.

Perhaps Hill invented SMART training because he also believed that creating a timeline and concrete plan were vital to the process. He does, however, take it a step further with daily affirmations. He believed that in order for your desire to remain a hot flame, you must always be connected to it. You need to write down your plan, with a concrete goal, and say it out loud twice a day. This keeps the words at the forefront of your mind.

Beyond Hill's tangible methods for success, keeping your desires burning is about stoking the flame with thoughts of your success. It is not good enough to say the words out loud, you need to feel it and live it all of the time. If you want to make a million dollars, you must feel that you already have it (minus the actual spending). You need to imagine yourself having what it is you desire.

What is interesting about Napoleon Hill's work is his fixation on riches. Now you can take this any way you want. Riches is really a vanilla word for anything that strikes your fancy. If money is really all you desire, go ahead and visualize yourself swimming in a pool of money. For the rest of us, I would suggest a life that is based on happiness and emotional well-being first. Following your intrinsic motivations will ultimately lead you to the life you are happiest with, doing things you love. Most of the time, this passion does lead to a monetary gain in the end, if you are diligent enough to find ways to get it.

This is the first time I will mention the idea of teamwork, and it probably won't be the last. Napoleon Hill brings up the notion that we are stronger in numbers. He recommends building a mastermind group of people that can all challenge and help each other learn and grow. Together, you can accomplish much more work in smaller amounts of time. That being said, you need to be very careful who you decide to form this with.

A member of your mastermind group must be willing to be part of a partnership, and you must be too. Neither can be selfish in the dividends and can't withhold information for their gains only. If you don't feel comfortable with this principle, scale it back. At the very least, ask for help in reaching your goals. You don't know everything, so when questions come up, don't be afraid to ask someone who does know for advice. For example, if you are starting a business and don't know how to file your taxes, seek the help of an accountant. That's it. Don't waste time trying to figure it out on your own. Let someone do those things you don't want to do, or don't have time to do, while you work on the big picture stuff.

The Takeaway

- Success is about balancing intrinsic and extrinsic motivation.

- Intrinsic motivation is that which comes from within.
- Extrinsic motivation is what drives you from outside to get things done.
- Stoke the fire of your desire by clearly defining what it is you want, then planning to get there.

FIVE

DEVELOPING A WARRIOR MINDSET, SELF-DISCIPLINE, AND UNBREAKABLE HABITS

> *You can't become committed or consistent with a weak mind. How many workouts have you missed because your mind, not your body, told you you were tired? How many reps have you missed out on because your mind said, "Nine reps is enough. Don't worry about the tenth." Probably thousands for most people, including myself. And 99% are due to weakness of the mind, not the body.*
>
> DREW SHAMROCK

WHAT DOES it mean to have a warrior mindset? As we look at history, we find that successful people in any field have all had the same things in common: creativity, tenacity, and self-discipline. Without these three things, we are weak and often fail to reach our full potential. Warriors have these traits all the time. They are constantly driven, never letting up. This is how they get so much done. You must be able to overcome procrastination and obstacles to get work done. No matter what field of interest you are in, or what area you decide to enter, the warrior mindset will have you accomplishing those goals faster than expected.

That being said, commitment and self-discipline are learned skills. We can all say that we have committed to something in the past, but over time, sometimes just a few days, the shininess of the end goal wears off as you wade through the weeds. Sticking to your guns is very difficult long term, and it takes a great deal of discipline to fight through the tough times.

Self-discipline comes down to one-part motivation and desire, one-part impulse control. That is, you need to fight the urge to get off track as a sacrifice to the ultimate goal. It is not enough to want to be there, you need to want to be there long term. For example, let's say you decide to go back to school. The draw here will be the ability to advance your career and earn more money in the future.

Your first week of classes is exciting, and you really feel you are getting somewhere. After a few weeks, the novelty wears off. What keeps you from quitting?

There are extrinsic motivators involved, like pressure from your peers, or the fact that you already paid for the whole semester. You also have the intrinsic motivation of bettering your life on your side as well.

Self-discipline will need to be the third factor to keep you going. More often than not, people who go back to school work during the day and attend class at night. It will be that discipline that drives you to school instead of home and lay on the couch for the rest of the day. This discipline is learned and cultivated.

If self-discipline has been a problem for you in the past, don't worry. There are actionable steps you can take today to brush up on your skills. First, remove all distractions. No matter what your task is, clear your schedule around it. Put your cell phone on silent, avoid going on social media or checking your email. All of these things occupy our brain's pleasure centers and make it impossible to get work done.

Next, keep yourself accountable by making daily, or even hourly, lists of things you want to accomplish. I would recommend blocking out your day as morning and afternoon, with a break in the middle. If your mind tends to wander, break it down even further. For example, between nine and eleven, you will work on a term paper. In that time, you will research and create an outline for what you will write about. Between ten and eleven, you will read the required chapters for tomorrow's class. Take a break for lunch and relaxation at noon, then get back to it at one. Plan your afternoon using the same breakdown techniques.

Self-discipline is best done a little bit at a time. It is much easier to convince yourself to study for an hour or to read one chapter than it is to say you need to study all day. This is too overwhelming for the brain to consider, and most likely anything learned after the first hour or two will be forgotten anyway. Keep your mind sharp and interested by adding variety to your day. Split your time between working on the computer, reading, meeting with clients, and free time accordingly.

Research has shown that people who actively work for less time during the day actually get more done. The threshold is about five hours per day. During this time, people are much more focused and have better work quality because their mind is sharper. Keep this fact in mind when creating any plan for yourself. For example, if you are going back to school on weeknights, don't plan to get all of your homework done on Saturdays. Schedule in a little time (even fifteen minutes) every day to study and work on assignments. This can easily be done at the tail end of your lunch break at work.

For self-discipline to work, there must be rules in place. Saying you will study an hour every day means very little. Saying that you will study for twenty minutes while eating lunch, and forty minutes before bed gives you a tangible, manageable goal (SMART). Remove obstacles from your day by eliminating habits that don't serve you well. For example, you will have plenty of time to study if you cut back watching television. Even more time can be dedicated to productive things if you cut it out altogether. Again, make sure to leave some leisure time in your schedule to avoid brain overload.

The magic word when it comes to self-discipline is accountability. This is a strong word and can be very difficult to achieve. You need to be true to yourself and consistent with your values and goals. You need to be able to mentally check in with yourself at any given moment and not feel guilty about your progress. If you do, it is likely because you are not reaching your goals and responsibilities.

Just as with motivation, there are extrinsic and intrinsic forms of accountability. Intrinsic is much less common than extrinsic, but certainly, holds more value. If you can justify the reasons why you do things well enough that you are motivated and accountable all on your own, you are golden. Keep it up.

There will be times that remaining accountable to something outside yourself can back you up. Perhaps your reason for going back to school is to help your spouse with the monthly bills. You want to contribute half to feel like an equal partner, and your spouse needs your support. Skipping class and assignments will have an equal effect on them. At least, if you put your goals out in the open for others to hear, a pressure to follow through emerges for the sake of your appearance and status to others. If you don't want to be viewed as a failure, you will follow through on your word. Build a team of supportive people around you to pick up when your discipline is waning.

Self-discipline can be learned by forming small habits. Just as we discussed with the SMART technique, you must set small, manageable goals for yourself to be successful. Transforming bad habits into good ones, and building upon existing good habits is called habit stacking. By changing a few minute things in your daily routine, you free up extra time and use that free time to make improvements. It can be used for studying, meditating, researching your next business move, just about anything. As I'm sure you've tried to change habits before, this is not so easy.

The good news is, it has been scientifically proven that the brain can change the way it thinks by building new neuronal pathways to different responses. For example, a person who is addicted to cigarettes can reshape their brain's response to stress. Instead of reaching for a cigarette, they can retrain it to chew a piece of gum. While this sounds simple, it does take a great deal of time and repetition.

Let's do a little science experiment. Charles Duhigg, Pulitzer Prize-winning reporter and author of *The Power of Habit* describes the "cue routine reward" system. That is, for every habit, good or bad, there is a similar habit loop. It is our job to figure out what cues trigger our habits, and how this habit rewards us in the end.

For example, if you are a smoker, the cue for smoking is usually a stressor, like a tough day at work. The habit is smoking, which is rewarded with a swift dose of nicotine to the brain, and the corresponding happy mood afterward. Since there will always be stress, the cycle repeats on an endless loop. The key to stopping any habit from happening is identifying the cue and rerouting the habit.

As with smoking, you need to make a conscious effort to pick a new habit when you feel cued to smoke by stress. Fighting the willpower of the brain (and the addictive nature of nicotine) makes this difficult to do, but it is certainly possible with repetition.

The same cycle happens in the brain with success and failure. You may notice that you tend to shy away from trying new things and being up in front of people. Pretend you are a renowned expert in your field. You write papers and develop experiments with ease, but the thought of talking about it in front of people scares you to death. The cue is the invitation to present your findings, the habit is to make an excuse to get out of it, and the reward is another day not having to face your fear.

Your brain is causing your limited potential. You may already be renowned in your field, but if you are not out there showing your stuff, that is all you will ever be. You are being limited by something that can be fixed very simply using this principle. When you think about it this way, it seems so simple. Fix the reaction to the cue, and move along with your day. And it is. If you tell yourself to change the reaction to the cue from a "no" to a "yes" and actually follow it, it can be that simple. Yes, this does challenge your inner logic, but if you make the situation black and white, it gives your brain a concise way to think. You may also use it in one of the following ways:

- To counteract social anxiety, always say yes to invitations to try new things.
- In building your business, systematically follow up with a phone call to every business card you receive at marketing events.
- When your alarm goes off at 5 am, you will get up, and not hit snooze.

- You will spend half your lunch break eating and the other half running through notes.

Building habits and having routines in place actually rests your mind. Have you ever driven to work, thought about other things and aren't really sure how you got there? If your brain is not taxed doing routine things, it has more ability for higher thinking, like coming up with your next dazzling business move.

Many articles have been written about the routines of highly successful people, and what they all have in common is consistency. They take time to do their have-to's, like answering emails, block out time for brainstorming and quiet time, and accomplishing their most daunting tasks early on in the day. Nobody will have the routine, but take steps to start building yours. Make a list of the things you need to do to get out of the house, then do them in order. Streamline the process to find more time. Do what works best for you and experiment to find the best routine of habits. You will be thankful you did.

The Takeaway

- You must develop your warrior mindset through self-discipline.
- Define the obstacles standing between you and your goals, and find ways around them.
- Be accountable to yourself first, but also find support around you to stay motivated.
- Reverse bad habits by recognizing your cue habit reward loops.
- Build good routines to help get the have-to's done.

PART THREE

CHALLENGE

SIX

STEPPING OUT OF YOUR COMFORT ZONE

> *It was a high counsel that I once heard given to a young person, "Always do what you are afraid to do."*
>
> RALPH WALDO EMERSON

Going for your goals will always require doing things you are uncomfortable doing. Believe me, there are obstacles in life that can only be tackled by doing something you have never done. This may mean taking a class you never saw yourself in, pushing yourself to visit that last client, despite your fatigue. Whatever the case may be, the only way to learn and grow is to get out of your comfort zone and own it.

Think about the human stage of growth. At first, we crawl, then we walk, then we run. The only way we can excel to running is by first crawling, determining this isn't good enough, and begin working on walking. That baby is unsteady on his feet, wishing to hold onto things for stability until finally, he is stable enough to walk on his own. This does not come with ease. In fact, it is usually met with crying and fussing.

When it comes to progress, we must push our boundaries. We need to face our fears and push past them to make any headway. For many people, this is the overwhelming prospect that holds them back. Others learn to embrace the fear and anxiety of being uncomfortable for the sake of progress.

For those of us on the fence, it is better to make small uncomfortable steps than to dive in head first. Moving across the country and starting a business is a big step and a lot of change all at once. A more conservative person would try and start a business where they are, where they are already comfortable. There is nothing wrong with either method, to each his own.

However, the only way to build mental toughness is to regularly do things that make you uncomfortable. This could be getting on the phone with clients, reaching out to new contacts, marketing or public speaking. When it comes to health, taking a class you have heard about or advancing to running instead of walking will put you out of your comfort zone. Whatever the case may be, we become stronger each and every time we decide to defy our comfort and strike out past the fences.

Change is just about the scariest thing out there, and this stems from the fear of the unknown. Our minds like to be content and comfortable with what is familiar. We are generally predictable, and unless we are pushed by some outside force, are usually content living out our normal routine forever. Going off course stresses the brain to think harder than normal, causing discomfort. The good news is, we can learn to be more resilient to change with some training.

Taking small action steps every day can get us used to making changes, and make it a little more comfortable each time. The same thing goes for risk, which, depending on your task of choice, could involve change as well. Yes, this process will be uncomfortable, that is the point. What we gain is the ability to be more versatile, and more able to deal with change gracefully, instead of fighting it tooth and nail.

The difference between successful people and those that are stuck is the ability to push past fear, accept change and do things outside of their comfort zone. There are a number of ways we can strike out of this zone every day. Challenge yourself to pick something from these examples, or from your own to-do list that will make you uncomfortable. The caveat here is that some things are uncomfortable because they are morally wrong, so it is important to do things that are ethical, but just personally uncomfortable to you. I feel like that should be a no-brainer, but you never know.

Exercise is a great place to develop mental toughness. Pushing yourself physically requires your brain to allow your body to move. If you are used to walking, it will be quite a leap to begin running. What makes it easier is focusing on your breath. Likely, your legs can handle the stress, and your lungs can too, but only if you control your breathing consciously. Focusing on getting full breaths in and out instead of panting takes mental toughness and focus. Many runners feel they enter a Zen-like state when they run, as their mind is totally engrossed in their breath, and nothing else.

The same thing goes for strength training. Our minds are good at telling us when to stop doing something for fear of fatigue or pain. Lifting weights that are safely beyond our muscle capacity helps build the muscle mass and strength, but only if our minds can handle the reps. It takes a bit of convincing to keep focused on the task and not give up.

Building mental toughness at work is necessary to your overall success. How many days have you wasted looking at social media or procrastinating in other ways? Did you feel accomplished at the end of the day? Likely not. Being more productive comes down to training your brain and coaxing it to stay focused.

Try to plan your day out ahead of time, blocking off specific amounts of time to complete tasks. Giving yourself a timeline to finish something puts pressure on you, giving the mind a reason to focus and get things done. Rewarding yourself in between tasks is a great way to stay focused. For example, give yourself an hour to finish a presentation, then take a break and have a snack. After the next task, take a quick brisk walk to replenish oxygen in the brain and get ready for the next thing.

If you have your eyes set on starting a business, getting your ideas together into workable tasks requires a huge amount of focus and mental toughness. I often see my lofty thoughts as wispy clouds swirling around above my head. They are out of reach as there are too many to focus on at once. There are marketing ideas, administrative thoughts, big dreams and little dreams. Taking the time to pull down a thought and develop it individually builds the toughness and allows you to make sense of it.

Take some time every day, even a few times a day, to focus on a thought, and think it through to completion. Writing things down can help you create a task list to carry the thought into action, that will eventually lead you to opening up your business and being a success. Doing so also increases your self-confidence, as you feel you have a clearer path to success.

Here are some little things you can do every day to start breaking your cycle of comfort. Challenge yourself to complete one of these things (or an idea of your own), every day. These things aren't that scary, so it shouldn't be so hard to accomplish. Just remember that the point is to be uncomfortable. If you aren't, you're not challenging yourself enough. With challenge comes growth:

- Take a different route to work
- Get coffee at a new coffee shop today
- Wear something you have never worn
- Rearrange the furniture in your home or office
- Create a new morning routine
- Wake up earlier
- Strike up a conversation on the bus
- Try a new exercise class
- Start a new exercise routine
- Schedule a presentation at your office to show off your skills
- Volunteer for a project at work instead of waiting to be assigned
- Volunteer in your community
- Listen to a different type of music
- Watch a video or webinar on a topic that is brand new to you

- Study concepts in your field that you don't know much about

---

AT THIS POINT, you may be asking why doing these seemingly menial tasks can help you forward your progress to success. The answer is very simple. Correct me if I'm wrong, but since you are reading this book, you are likely stuck in a comfort circle. That is, you are spinning around, doing what is already in your wheelhouse. You are comfortable here, like a big fish in a little pond.

The only way to break that cycle is to start branching out beyond that circle. Starting with small task such as this makes the discomfort a bit more bearable. Over time, you will master the small stuff, and challenge yourself to broaden your circle even more. Take for example, Richard Branson. He is assumed to be worth almost five billion dollars, and owns Virgin, a company famous for its involvement in business, but also branches out into hundreds of other ventures, including air travel and space exploration.

What many people don't know is that Branson has a learning disability, and dropped out of high school to start his first business. Nobody thought he would succeed due to his dyslexia, and yet he is more successful than most people out there. He dedicates his success to the ability to delegate tasks (like reading) to others while focusing on new projects. He gets a kick out of challenging himself and the proof is in his business growing way beyond its initial business model.

We are only limited by the size of our comfort zone. Nothing extraordinary ever comes from playing safely within your comfort zone. Strike out and begin to challenge yourself each and every day. Eventually, you will crave a new challenge and will shy away from doing the same old thing. This is a cornerstone of success.

The Takeaway

- Nothing extraordinary happens from your comfort zone
- Challenge yourself to do something you are uncomfortable with every day

SEVEN

DEALING WITH FAILURES AND BECOMING MORE RESILIENT

> *Life has no smooth road for any of us; and in the bracing atmosphere of a high aim, the very roughness stimulates the climber to steadier steps, till the legend, over steep ways to the stars, fulfills itself.*
>
> W. C. DOANE

WHILE THIS BOOK has been largely focused on bringing you up and preparing you for success, we need to talk about failure. Everybody fails. Those who say they never fail are either lying or never step far enough out of their comfort zone to take a risk. Challenging yourself to go bigger and better comes with risks, and sometimes things don't work out.

. . .

FAILURE IS A FUNNY WORD. It implies that nothing was gained from your efforts. In science, there are no failed experiments. There are only experiments that prove or disprove your theory. While pride can sometimes get in the way, you have still learned something that can value your field. You now know that one theory has been disproven, leading you closer to finding one that actually works. Did you know that Thomas Edison conducted thousands of failed experiments before perfecting the light bulb?

Failure is only true failure if you don't learn from your mistakes. Being arrogant and trying to cover up for your unsuccessful ventures doesn't help you learn and grow. Instead of pushing an event to the past and trying to forget about it, keep it present, pick it apart, and suck all of the knowledge out of it that you possibly can. Failure happens when you continue to make the same mistakes over and over again, having gained nothing from the experience.

LET'S say you just had your first official business meeting for your new company yesterday. You pitched your product to your very first client, and you bombed the presentation. Nobody was interested in the product, nobody asked questions, and the sale did not happen. You have three choices: give up the business completely because nobody likes you, continue unsuccessfully with the same sales pitch, or find out what went wrong and fix it. Successful people are able to withstand the criticism and make the most out of a negative situation by learning. Granted, this can be a downright gut-wrenching process when you thought so clearly that your business would succeed. It will be difficult, but in the long run, pushes you a step closer to success.

Many successful people have said that it was a rejection or failure that gave them the motivation necessary to move forward and prove people wrong. This need to succeed is something we are all born with, yet many of us give up on it as the road gets rough. Being mentally tough and fighting through the criticism and humbly learning your lessons hones your skills well enough to succeed. Getting through these moments with grace and dignity can be difficult, but there are a number of ways to get through it.

First, be flexible. Yes, you need to stay focused on your primary goal, but as you hit roadblocks, you need to be able to think on your feet and change your plan of action to keep moving forward. Think about the game of football. If the team runs the ball and is immediately shut down by the other team's defenses, it is not wise to run the same play again. For example, since the business proposal you have been working on for weeks didn't go well, you cannot keep using the same process for sales. You need to give in and try something new. Don't be afraid to ask for help, even if that means asking the client outright what they did wrong.

A carefully worded question like, "What is holding you back from pulling the trigger today" can help pinpoint where your weak points are so that you may focus more on addressing that. Remember that some things you consider common sense as an expert in your field can often be lost on others. A deeper explanation could easily resolve the problem, even in time to close the sale.

Next, don't let yourself get paralyzed by rejection. An immediate reaction to being rejected is wanting to hide under your bed and never come out. Think about all of the time you have put into this venture. What about all of the motivation and stamina you have shown thus far? Are you willing to throw that all away? Take a few minutes to wallow, maybe even cry, then dust yourself off and start working on a new plan. One 'no' is never the end. Force yourself to be resilient and keep trying. Not only will you eventually hear 'yes' you will certainly impress lots of people by not giving up.

Having a good support network can mean the difference between giving up and keeping on. I just gave you a literary pep talk (you're welcome), but it often means more coming from a loved one. Having people who care about you in on your goals gives you something to fall back on as you are failing. Studies show that people who have a good support system often lose more weight than those striking out alone. Not only are they more accountable because someone else knows, they can be re-energized by the kind words of motivation their support system gives them. Falling on your face feels much better when a kind hand lifts you back up.

A great way to pick yourself up when you are down is to surround yourself with motivational media. YouTube has channels dedicated to self-help gurus and compiles words of wisdom from some of the most successful people. Hearing about success and being mentally tough and dedicated lift your spirits and energize you. In fact, listening to this in the background on any given workday can help motivate you to work harder, longer and more efficiently. Take a few minutes in your morning, at lunch, and at your 2 pm slump to listen to material like this to keep the momentum going.

Having quotes by successful people all around you primes your success as well. Set something inspiring as your desktop background. Tape your mantra to the side of the computer screen, right alongside your goals and desires. Take a look every time you need to be reminded of your path.

Perhaps the most uplifting thing when you are down is hearing about the failure of other successful people. Keep in mind that all successful, famous, world-renowned people once came from humble roots. Besides the few that ride the coattails of their parents or siblings into the limelight, most of them were regular people with day jobs, growing up in mediocre or dismal environments, with people who thought they would grow up to be average.

That is hardly inspiring in the moment, but what is inspiring is the fact that these people defied all the odds, worked hard and eventually found success. That is, after all of their failures. Did you know that Babe Ruth held the world record for home runs, but also the record for number of strikeouts? This basically means he only succeeded half the time, yet found the notoriety anyway. Stephen King published his first book, Carrie, after being rejected over twenty times. He nearly gave up.

You will fail. Don't let it become the reason you did not continue your path to success. Be resilient, rely on the support system you have built around you and find ways that work to motivate you. The setbacks you face have been put there to challenge you, to hone your skills and act as learning opportunities. Do yourself a favor and consider every setback a lesson. Find the titbit of information you were meant to learn, and use it. Being afraid to fail means you will not take the risks necessary for success.

The Takeaway

- Setbacks are inevitable, handling them with grace is a sign of success.
- Surround yourself with a good support network to lift you up when you fall.
- Look at the success stories of others and see that they have once failed too.

PART FOUR

CONFIDENCE

EIGHT
THE IMPORTANCE OF SELF-CONFIDENCE AND SELF-BELIEF

> *Self-confidence is the first requisite to great undertakings.*
>
> SAMUEL JOHNSON

IN ORDER TO achieve the success you have always dreamed of, you must believe, wholeheartedly, that you can do it. I know this can be very difficult to do, as pulling confidence out of nowhere seems nearly impossible. However, we have already seen the success of others, and how they were once in a position similar to yours. It is possible, it is just a matter of building strong self-confidence in order to push through those tough times.

Believing in yourself is a learned skill. I believe we are born thinking we can do just about anything. When we are young, we cry our eyes out to get our way. We defy our parent's orders and run after what we want. As we age, we become more conditioned to follow the rules and behave ourselves. What this gets us is a well-behaved child that grows into a law-abiding citizen that leads a mediocre existence. For the record, being a law-abiding citizen in the literal sense is great, but what I really mean is that they follow all the rules, even the ones that can be bent. We become conditioned to follow the same path others have taken in front of us, never daring to try something new, and this is a mistake.

If you have a dream to do something different, you need to believe in your idea and trust your instincts well enough to go after it. You need to be tough, facing your critics and resilient to get back up when you have failed. Without self-confidence, you will more than likely fail.

If you are starting today from a point of general low self-esteem, let's work on it. Taking time for targeted self-care each and every day can help build your confidence. Recite positive affirmations to yourself every day. Give yourself a pep-talk whenever you are feeling blue. Stop comparing yourself to the likes of others. Remember, you are trying to do something new, there is no comparing your success to that of anyone else.

That goes for appearance too. So many people get

bogged down in the idea of beauty standards. Saying things like, "If I could lose this weight, I could conquer the world" are really detrimental to progress and really only serve procrastination. You can conquer the world regardless of body size, but if it would make you feel more confident, take steps to change.

Focus on the small things. I have said many times that looking at the big picture all at once is overwhelming. You cannot tackle everything you want to do all at once, so pick the low-lying fruit, start with the easy stuff and go from there. Every little accomplishment adds self-confidence points to your score, priming you for more.

You are your own worst enemy, remember that. The only thing that is limiting you from living the life you want is yourself. Once you are out of your own way, the sky is the limit. Unfortunately, many of us fall victim to self-sabotage, the act of maliciously deterring yourself from success. This is often seen in weight loss, as people underlyingly fear what change comes from losing weight. That fear of change transcends all areas of self-improvement.

We need to learn to recognize the self-sabotaging behavior, like making self-defeating statements, downplaying your skills and procrastinating. If you find yourself putting a negative spin on things, like focusing on all of your failures, you may be self-sabotaging. Do you reach goals then often back away from them? This happens often in weight loss. People reach their goal but backslide, either due to failure maintaining the lifestyle, or because they don't feel they are worthy of the success.

The first step to counteracting self-sabotage is recognizing it as it comes up. If you find yourself doing any of the things mentioned above, start tracking it. Write things down in a journal to identify triggers and cues for this behavior. Once that is done, you can begin working to change your thought patterns, much as we did with the cue, habit, reward training discussed earlier.

This can be a pretty simple process, depending on the problem. If you think negatively, simply think positive. Instead of highlighting all that went wrong, look at what had gone right first. Sure, you need to figure out how to improve for the future, but focusing on that negativity does nothing but bring you down.

You may also guide yourself solely on your past. Saying things like, 'could have' or 'should have' are useless. The past cannot be changed. Bad things happen, and we can't make our future choices out of fear of repeating history. For example, having had a relationship that ended badly does not mean that a new one will fail. If you did make mistakes, you can focus on correcting them, but take the risk just the same.

Do you settle? Is that the job you really want? Do you still wish you were ten pounds lighter? Is this where you want to be? If you can honestly answer 'yes' to all of these questions, you probably shouldn't be reading this book. Now if you were to be completely sincere, there is probably something you have settled for. Settling means that you have given up and lowered your standards to make things easier. That may be hard to hear, but it is the truth. Take some time to think about what you may have settled for and raise your standards. Go after what you wanted to begin with. Don't settle, you are worth the effort!

Another big one is procrastination. You are capable of some quality work but by waiting until the last minute, you end up rushing around and doing an average job. Your potential is being squandered by your own mind. Stop blaming the obstacles in your way and start earlier. Make a step-by-step plan for yourself and get cracking.

Some of the most successful people make daily affirmations. To be honest, the first time I was told to say something positive to myself in the mirror, I laughed. This is quite sad, since making yourself feel good should really be a top priority. Yes, you may feel a bit silly the first few times you do it, and this is a sign of low self-confidence.

Making daily affirmations is one of the simplest,

least time-consuming ways to boost your confidence. First, pick a phrase. It has to be something that really hits home with you and your goals. For example, if getting healthy is your goal, affirming that you have the ability to do it is a good start. You can also use quotes from people that inspire you or do something generic like, "I am smart, I am strong, I am capable of whatever comes my way". Here are a few more to get you started:

- I am creative, self-reliant and resilient in everything I do.
- I can solve problems. No challenge is too large for me to handle.
- I am confident, capable and well-kept. Nothing is standing in my way.

If none of these speak to you, think about it this way. Think of the future when you have reached your goal and found success. Imagine that you are being interviewed by a reporter, and the question is about your tips to help others reach success. What would you say the biggest drivers for your success were? Taking time for yourself? Helping others? What kind of daily affirmation would you imagine that successful you use? What kind of advice would future you give for success?

If affirmations don't seem to work, keep trying

them. In the meantime, try a few other simple things to automatically boost your confidence.

Sit up straight: Good posture makes you look more confident to others as well as provides the 'backbone' to keep your body healthy and agile.

Dress for success: The old advice of dressing for the job you want comes in handy here. If you look the part, you will have the confidence to act the part.

Speak clearly and concisely: Thinking before you speak and saying exactly what you mean will open doors for you.

Stand up for yourself: If you believe in yourself, you should have no problem advocating for yourself when your ethics are on trial.

Organize yourself and your space: Just knowing where everything is, gives you the confidence that you can carry out a task with ease. Besides, looking for things before starting a project is an exhausting waste of time.

Often times, the best way to boost self-confidence is to gain it from others. People who are confident exude their confidence, and it is an energy that can be felt. Just being around people who believe in themselves and their causes is contagious. Unfortunately, negative environments with self-sabotaging people are easier to find than healthy ones focused on growth. Luckily, we have the internet for that. Articles abound about the successes of others and their words of wisdom. Taking a daily dose of positivity and wise words from those who have found their confident place help to find yours.

Take a look at what some famous people have said about their success. Most times, it is all about confidence and finding that place. First, look at Jerry Seinfeld. In his early days as a stand-up comedian, he found that his jokes kept getting better and better if he made the commitment to write each and every day. He made a game out of it by buying a big wall calendar that showed the whole year right in front of him. Each day he worked on his material he could have the satisfaction of marking a big red 'X' over that day. He would become addicted to this, keeping up his commitment every day to ensure that he didn't break the chain.

You may not decide to be a stand-up comic but using this practice, or something very similar to track your progress gives a small, tangible goal to meet every day. Make a similar goal to do some task every day and track your success. You will be a bit disappointed when you miss a day, driving you to do the work.

A number of successful people, including Richard Branson, Oprah Winfrey, and Donald Trump live by a similar motto. That is, don't give up. Never give up. Let that be your absolute. Life is not black and white, but this resolve can be. Simply keep trying. Each and every time you fail, take some time to reflect and move on. Building that resolve and mental tenacity will bring you success.

The Takeaway

- Self-confidence is a learned skill that can be developed by devoting time to your inner workings.

- Daily affirmations may seem silly, but repeating them, as well as saying your goals out loud makes the brain believe what it hears.

- Stay positive and thwart self-sabotage.

- Everyone fails. It is what you decide to do afterward that makes or breaks you.

NINE
VISUALIZATION, POSITIVE THINKING, JOURNALING, & MEDITATION

> *Visualize this thing that you want, see it, feel it, believe in it. Make your mental blueprint, and begin to build.*
>
> ROBERT COLLIER

GETTING your mind where it needs to be for success is quite a task. We have already discussed building self-confidence and self-discipline in the course of improving mental toughness. But where does the strength to do all of these things come from?

We each have an inner energy, a fire, that can either be inflamed or extinguished. Those who have given up could visualize their flame as just a small ember with nothing around to kindle it. Others keep their flame burning hot and high, constantly fueling it.

How can we go from having a small ember to a hot white flame of motivation, desire, and tenacity? We need to work on our mental health.

Now, when I hear mental health, I usually associate that with anxiety or depression, which is involved. But let us focus on the broader definition of the term, which involves the need to actively maintain our mind. Just like we engage in regular physical activity to keep our bodies in shape, we also need to do things to relax our minds, build our thinking power and build our prowess. We can do this through meditation, journaling and challenging our brain. In order to move forward with our goals, we need to visualize our success and think positively. We need to do these things on a regular basis as preventative maintenance, and it must not fall by the wayside.

First, let's talk preventative maintenance via meditation. This practice is just that: something you get better at the more you do it. Meditation has been around for many centuries, with its origins in Asia. The goal of meditation is to clear the mind of all of the jumbled thoughts we think in order to start again fresh. This is accomplished first by clearing the mind and giving little notice to the thoughts that sneak in and out.

Meditation can be done just about anywhere, but if you are just starting out, your best bet is to find a quiet room with dim lighting and rid yourself of distractions. Close the door and don't bring your computer or phone with you. The room should be in comfortable temperature and you can choose to sit on the floor, in a chair, on the bed, or in any position that is comfortable.

Next, sit quietly, close your eyes and focus on your breath. With each inhale, imagine that a steady stream of energy is filling your lungs. Feel it spread throughout your body, to each fingertip, down to your toes. As you exhale, imagine all of the pent-up, negative energy rushing out of your body. Continue breathing, focusing only on this sensation.

Many people can enter a good meditative state by focusing on their breath alone. The problem is, we have a hard time shutting off our brains, so we often get sidetracked and lose focus on the breath. If this sounds like you, try chanting a word to yourself either inside your head or out loud. This gives you something more to focus and may keep your attention better.

If you can't focus on something, don't call that a failure. Thoughts are likely to slip in and out of your meditation, especially as you begin to practice. Instead of trying to shoo them away, let them float in and out on their own. As they float by, don't give them any attention. That is if you are thinking about what else you need to do to finish a project, don't elaborate, and don't give any sort of emotion to it. Just sit with the thought, and naturally let it flow out on its own. Don't worry, it will still be there when you are done.

There is no set time for meditation, although giving it at least fifteen to twenty minutes to start will give your mind a chance to get with the program, with some time left for the real benefit. My best advice would be to go in with an open mind. If you are skeptical about the practice, push that aside and give it a good shot. Try practicing every day. As Jerry Seinfeld would do, keep track of this habit by marking down the days you do it, as well as how you feel afterward. Building habits takes time, so make sure to give it your best effort.

If you want, incorporate journaling into your meditation practice. After you have cleared and focused your mind, take just a few minutes to jot down some thoughts. This can be anything from a grocery list, to-do list once you begin working, or something more substantial, like how the meditation made you feel, and what other emotions are going on.

Journaling helps us make sense of our thoughts and emotions. If you are on a journey to meet a goal that requires a lot of attention, you are likely feeling stressed, anxious and afraid that you might fail. Instead of living with these emotions, writing about them can help bring them into the light so that you might do something about them.

Journaling can also be used throughout the day to

counteract your negative thoughts. Remember that cue, habit, reward idea we talked about earlier? Being more conscious of your negative thoughts can help you pinpoint triggers for them. For example, as you near the end of a long workday, you tend to have more negative thoughts. Sure, you may feel a bit accomplished for what you have done, but your brain also gets tired. In that moment, negative thoughts about giving up and quitting rear their ugly head. As you are faced with planning your next day, sometimes the brain likes to throw you a curve and say, "Wouldn't it just be easier to quit?"

Instead of just pushing through these feelings, write those thoughts down and understand that the main reason you are thinking them is because of fatigue. Tomorrow, after you have had a good night's sleep to recharge your batteries, you will be ready to tackle this to-do list.

Once you can identify where you are having negative thoughts, it will be possible to transform them into positive thoughts. The brain is an amazing organ, but it is just tissue and nerves, just like the rest of the body. The brain forms thought patterns that are connected directly between an outside stimulus, like seeing a tennis ball, and the memory tissue that can identify that it is yellow. Repeat behaviors create superhighways of nerve tissue in order to reach this result faster.

We can see this evidence in the development of fine motor skills. Babies develop the ability to chew, but not necessarily feed themselves. As they see the parent feed them from a bowl over and over, they develop the motor skills to do it themselves, until they have mastered it.

Negative thoughts are just the same. If you had failed a test in the past, taking it again will bring back feelings of self-doubt and sadness. Your brain has seen this situation before and makes sense of it the same way it had in the past for the sake of simplicity. It wants to arrive at the quickest answer possible. Fortunately, it is also possible to repave these neuronal superhighways to include different outcomes. For example, thinking about the test you failed in a more positive light, the resulting thoughts change forever. Seeing the retest as a second chance is positive. Knowing that you have studied is also positive.

This works very well with building your self-confidence. If you are hard on yourself about your weight or appearance, every time you look in the mirror will remind you of that negativity. Using positive self-talk and affirmations gives your brain something to focus on instead. Instead of thinking that you look fat in this outfit, say out loud how nice the color looks against your skin. Each and every time you have a negative thought (that you can recognize), consciously make the effort to balance it out with something positive.

Finally, in order to get anywhere with your goals, you must visualize it. You need to see, through your mind's eye, what it is that you want. When you can put a picture, a feeling, even a smell (say you want to open a bakery) to your goal, it puts the process in motion. Visualizing your goals keeps it forever fresh in your mind, and gives you the motivation to carry it out.

Visualization can be done on its own, or in the process of meditation, although practicing visualization takes a bit more effort. Much like meditation, find a quiet place to sit comfortably. Close your eyes and focus on the breath. Calm your mind and clear your head for just a few minutes.

Before anything else comes to mind, think about your goal. For the sake of example, say that you *do* want to open a bakery. Imagine that the chair you are sitting in is the one that graces your new office. Feel the back of the chair against your skin. Feel the weight of your body against its seat.

Imagine the computer screen in front of you. It is opened up to your website page. See the bright colors and funky font you picked to represent your business. Visualize a customer counter at the bottom of the screen, quickly ticking upward as your online sales come flying in. Smile to yourself. This is what it feels like to be successful.

Next, turn your attention to the door. Waft weightlessly out the door out to the kitchen. Feel the wave of oven warmth on your face and the smell of sweet lemon cake in your nose. Breathe it in. Watch as your happy, busy employees flit around, assembling cakes, baking cookies, and piping frosting.

Continue on to the sales floor, where happy customers come up and thank you for opening your business. Look at the beautiful, shiny glass cases that hold your prized desserts, with the kids' faces eyeing all of their favorites. Imagine how wonderful it will feel to have this success.

Open your eyes. Now is the time for the real work to begin. You have imagined the space, your office, the kitchen, the sales floor. Now bring it into reality. Turn each and every aspect into a to-do list for yourself, from the shiny new mixers to the glass cases.

Visualizing this way brings more reality to your dream. Use this technique, as well as meditation and journaling to sort through your thoughts and turn them into actionable things. You can do it, and these techniques will help!

The Takeaway

- Good mental health aids the process of reaching your goals.
- Nurture your mind through meditation, calming those thoughts to bring focus.
- Journaling helps make sense of feelings and negative thoughts so that they may be dealt with.
- Visualize your dreams with guided imagery to help sort through your goal and bring more clarity.

CONCLUSION

Now that we have reached the end of this book, it is time to get started on your journey. This text has equipped you with the tools and skills necessary to be successful at just about any venture. You have already taken the step to make improvements to propel your venture, so you are in good shape.

Mental toughness is a learned skill. Practicing these skills is the only way to improve and make progress. Take some time to write down your goals using the SMART technique, and build a list of small tasks you can complete to bring this goal to fruition.

Remember that success is a result of hard work, mental toughness, and a desire to succeed. Don't get bogged down in the details. Most importantly, never give up. If you do, what will you do with the time you have left?

2. OVERCOMING SOCIAL ANXIETY

THE 30-DAY CHALLENGE TO BUILD CONFIDENCE AND OVERCOME SOCIAL ANXIETY

INTRODUCTION

Have you ever found yourself in a position wherein all you wanted was for the ground to swallow you whole? Or have you experienced moments in which you desperately wanted to go home and lock yourself in your room? Do you avoid office parties? Do you get irritated when other people try to make small talk when you just want to mind your own business?

If your answer is 'yes' to any or all of these questions, you are not alone. I have personally experienced situations in which I felt panic and anxiety just being around other people. There were times when I got anxious while thinking about an upcoming event and imagining what it's going to be like when the date finally arrives.

I lived alone and my home was my comfort zone. I did not want to travel to far locations, and I definitely did not want to meet new people. Moreover, there were instances wherein I completely avoided the attention of others. I avoided going to crowded places, starting a conversation with anyone, and even being active on social media.

I avoided huge family gatherings and reunions because I didn't like being around relatives whom I do not really know. And even though I talked to close family members and friends, I chose not to tell them everything. Opening up to people has never been my cup of tea. I felt comfortable and at ease when I was isolated – far away from the rest of the world. I had social anxiety.

It's Harmless, Right?

You may think that being socially isolated is alright. In fact, you might even prefer it because you're not interacting with anyone. Thus, you believe that you are not causing anyone else harm. Well, actually, you're wrong.

Social anxiety greatly influences people's overall quality of life. You're essentially denying yourself the opportunity to live a good life. You're hurting your family and close friends by not giving them attention and not spending time with them. You're harming everyone around you because your anxiety prevents you from functioning normally in society.

When you worry too much about what other people think, you deny yourself the opportunity to be free. Your fear of criticism, sarcastic and rude remarks, and negative attention will prevent you from doing anything truly worthwhile. Likewise, negative self-talk will keep you from reaching your full potential. In other words, you won't really be happy with social anxiety.

Finding the Solution

Truth be told, social anxiety is more than just paranoia and self-consciousness. It's a problem that needs to be solved, especially since it can leave a person paralyzed. Being someone who went through it all and succeeded, I felt that it's necessary to help those still finding their way out. That's why I decided to write this brief yet informative guide.

If you decide that you don't want to feel nerves in the social settings anymore and that you want to be in control of your own life, then this book is for you.

In this book, you will learn everything about social anxiety. You'll also see how it can affect your life. More importantly, you will discover the strategies and techniques that you can use to improve your condition. I encourage you to keep on reading and learning. As you go through every page, you increase your knowledge of this debilitating problem.

INTRODUCTION

The strategies and techniques mentioned in this book are backed by research. So, you can rest assured that you're in good hands. As the author of this book, I only have your best interest in mind. If you follow everything written here, you will gradually escape social anxiety's chains. Your condition will improve, and your attitude towards events and interactions will get better.

Keep in mind, however, that treating social anxiety begins with your own self. You have to be determined to get better. You have to decide that you no longer want to be in the dark. The first step to wellness is admitting that you have a problem and wanting to get better. Then, you have to make an effort to actually take the necessary steps.

Before we start, I have to point out that I'm not a qualified psychologist and the advice I provide in this book is only my opinion. However, as an individual who had lived with social anxiety, I think that my opinion is worth considering.

So, without further ado, let us dive right in!

PART ONE
UNDERSTANDING SOCIAL ANXIETY

ONE
WHAT IS SOCIAL ANXIETY?

Social anxiety disorder is also known as social phobia. It's the kind of anxiety disorder that leads to extreme fear and panic in social settings. It involves being too concerned about what others think, as well as worrying about being embarrassed or excluded.

The Anxiety and Depression Association of America (ADAA) reports that fifteen million Americans suffer from the disorder. In most cases, symptoms begin to appear at around thirteen years of age.

People experience social anxiety at different levels, but nearly everyone has experienced its symptoms at some point. Those who suffer from this disorder tend to experience difficulty dealing with other people. They find it hard to talk to others, meet new friends, and attend social gatherings. They don't like huge events where a lot of people are present. They also fear being scrutinized or judged by their peers. They may be aware that their fears and beliefs are irrational, but they still feel powerless against them.

Social anxiety isn't the same as shyness though, given that the former is debilitating and persistent.

To begin with, you need to know if you are suffering from social anxiety by asking yourself the following questions:

- Do you tend to reject invitations to social events?
- Do you tend to spend lunch break by yourself instead of sitting in the cafeteria with your peers or colleagues?
- Do you refuse to attend family reunions?
- Do you dislike meeting new people?
- Do you avoid engaging in small talk?
- Do you avoid eye contact with people?
- Do you dislike being the center of attention?
- Do you feel uncomfortable being watched by others as you do something?
- Do you avoid going to public toilets?
- Do you avoid drinking or eating in public places?
- Do you avoid making public speeches or speaking in front of an audience?

- Do you prefer to communicate via text messages or e-mails instead of phone calls?

If you answered 'yes' to a majority of these questions, then you may actually have a social anxiety disorder.

The good news is, social anxiety is a treatable condition, and many have had success in the past and I believe you will, too.

Now, let's take a look at some common symptoms of social anxiety.

The Takeaway

- Social anxiety can severely diminish the quality of your life by preventing you from attending social functions and mingling with other people.
- Social anxiety is not the same as shyness. It can be debilitating and persistent.

TWO
THE SYMPTOMS OF SOCIAL ANXIETY

RECALL the most recent social situation you were involved in. It could be a situation where you were called in class, a party with your co-workers or friends, or a family gathering.

What were your reactions?

Did you suddenly feel that you couldn't think anymore, your heart rate going up, and your hands sweating?

Well, these are all common physical symptoms of social anxiety.

The common physical symptoms of social anxiety include:

- Nausea
- Blushing
- Excessive sweating

- Shaking or trembling
- Shortness of breath
- Difficulty speaking
- Increased heart rate
- Lightheadedness or dizziness

While these symptoms are occasionally seen in people without the disorder, sufferers experience them more frequently and more intensely.

There are also psychological symptoms such as intense worry about social events, fear of humiliating oneself, and refusal to attend important gatherings. Likewise, those with the disorder may worry that others will notice their nervousness and even rely on alcohol to have the courage to face social situations.

Keep in mind that people with social anxiety don't merely avoid big events. They exert effort to minimize their chances of interacting with other people in all possible ways. They'll refrain from using public toilets and won't dare ask questions. Likewise, talking on the phone and dining in restaurants are things they'll rarely do – and they may have to be forced to engage in these activities.

The symptoms listed here, however, may not manifest in every situation. Some people have selective or limited anxiety. Their symptoms only occur whenever they do something in particular, such as speaking with strangers or eating in front of other people. Those who suffer from extreme cases of social anxiety tend to experience the symptoms in all kinds of social settings.

If you are suffering from social anxiety, you must know a lot of the symptoms listed above. But do you know what really causes you to act that way? Read the next chapter to find out.

The Takeaway

- Physical symptoms of social anxiety include nausea, blushing, excessive sweating, shaking, shortness of breath, difficulty speaking, increased heart rate...etc.
- Psychological symptoms of social anxiety generally involve excessive worrying about a social situation.

THREE
CAUSES OF SOCIAL ANXIETY

THERE's no denying that social anxiety is among the most complex disorders in existence. Those reactions in the brain are actually brought forth by a myriad of factors, ranging from the environmental to the biological. What makes things worse is that anxiety can have multiple roots. Here are some common causes of social anxiety:

Rough Upbringing

As they say, everything begins at home – even how you view other people's opinions. A child who grows up feeling loved, accepted, and liked, will develop a sense of self-worth and won't seek validation from others. On the other hand, growing up without getting appreciated or encouraged will create self-doubt. Distinguishing criticism from praise will become a challenge as well.

People who are socially anxious tend to make assumptions towards the way others see them. Note that how you were evaluated and perceived as you grew up have shaped your expectations in social encounters. So if your parents were too hard on you, feelings of inadequacy or rejection will linger. You may fear that others will see the very same problems your parents thought you had.

Negative Experiences

Certain experiences can have a lasting effect, causing distress years after they've occurred. Bullying, for example, is something that many social anxiety sufferers have gone through.

They still remember the days when they were beaten up in school or when they were humiliated in front of their friends. Simply put, moments that single out people as odd or unacceptable can make them prone to social anxiety.

Family conflict is another thing that counts as a negative experience. This isn't merely about problems caused by financial woes or disagreements in child discipline. Sibling rivalry, especially if you're the one who often gets the short end of the stick, can create problems that could very well last a lifetime. Note that the effect of family conflict doesn't end within the confines of one's home. Sometimes, it's the main factor that fuels bullying.

Major Life Changes

Major events, such as moving to a new city, getting divorced, or having a baby, can leave a significant impact on a person's mental state. They demand adaptation, which can take a lot of time and energy. Also, it's common for people to give all sorts of opinions during these events, regardless of whether their insights have been requested. Due to this, old vulnerabilities could resurface and new ones may develop.

Changes that come with life stages can cause social anxiety as well. For example, adolescence brings so many changes with it that many in that particular stage of life end up getting overwhelmed. Not only do adolescents have to adapt to their rapid growth and sexual development, but they also have to handle peer pressure and romantic interests. Their ever-growing independence complicates things further.

It's due to these that social anxiety or the symptoms associated with it usually manifest during the teenage years.

The Brain Structure

As you will discover in the next chapter, the amygdala plays an important role in processing the stress response. While social anxiety may be caused by irrational belief and perceived danger, it's possible that the problem itself is brought forth by an overactive amygdala. Simply put, even if there are minimal signals related to fear or danger, the brain structure hastily interprets the situation as life-threatening.

The amygdala's size is related to the likelihood of becoming overactive. Being larger strengthens its connections with structures that allow for emotion to be perceived and regulated. However, that also increases its likelihood of triggering a stress response. Experts from Stanford University have discovered that the degree of anxiety experienced on a daily basis can be predicted just by checking the amygdala's size.

Genetics and Heredity

The more sensitive you are to stress, the faster you see physiological changes whenever you're in stressful situations. Rapid breathing and elevated heart rate are two of the most common examples of these changes. To a certain extent, this sensitivity or reactivity is determined by your genetics. So, if someone in your family has social anxiety, it's not that surprising that you have it as well.

Susceptibility to brain imbalances and changes in neural activity can likewise be influenced by genes. This is something to be expected, given that many mental health conditions have genetic roots (depression and schizophrenia can both be passed down). Just to be clear, it's still possible to have social anxiety despite not having a family member afflicted with it.

Appearance Concerns

In some cases, social anxiety may stem from medical conditions and other related issues that affect appearance. For instance, those who've been involved in an accident and ended up suffering facial disfigurement may worry that they'll no longer be seen as normal. They may become too self-conscious, resulting in the disorder's development. People with conditions that affect movement and speech (such as Parkinson's) are at risk as well.

PROBLEMS CAN HAVE VARIOUS CAUSES, which can be difficult to disentangle. Nevertheless, it's possible to categorize these causes into two – stresses and vulnerability factors. Stresses refer to the demands of your life stage as well as the circumstances that affect you. Vulnerability factors, on the other hand, refer to long-standing traits that make you more susceptible. These are psychological and biological in nature.

In the next chapter, I want to discuss how Amygdala in our brain works and how it is related to social anxiety disorder.

The Takeaway

- Common causes of social anxiety include rough upbringing, negative experiences, major life changes, the brain structure, genetics and heredity and appearance concerns.
- We can categorize these causes into two – stresses and vulnerability factors.

FOUR
UNDERSTANDING WHAT GOES ON IN YOUR BRAIN

SOCIAL ANXIETY CAN BE BETTER understood by looking at how the brain works. To begin with, you have to understand a part of the brain's fear center, known as the **amygdala.**

Amygdala and its relation to the social anxiety

The amygdala, despite being a small structure within the brain, is known to affect emotion – and with that, it has influence over motivation as well as emotional behavior.

What's really interesting is that the amygdala serves as a link between structures that send sensory signals and those that interpret such signals. So, whenever there are signals indicative of a threat, it's the amygdala that initiates the stress response. You can see it as a 'danger detector' built within your brain.

What happens when the stress response is triggered? Basically, cortisol (a steroid hormone) and norepinephrine (an organic chemical) get secreted in increasing amounts. Together, the two improves reflexes and perception, as well as accelerates heart rate and blood flow – things that are crucial if you're indeed facing a dangerous situation. Of course, with your heightened awareness and increased speed comes to an even greater sense of fear and tension, supposedly better allowing you to either flee or fight.

In some situations, this warning is good because it actually allows you to remove yourself from the dangerous situation. This response protects you from getting seriously hurt or even killed.

To someone with the social anxiety, however, that perceived danger often involves the possibility of doing or experiencing something unpleasant during interactions with other people.

In other words, your brain or your subconscious mind tries to warn you about the possible danger even in situations that are not life-threatening. It perceives social settings as a threat or a danger. It believes that you are going to get rejected or embarrassed. It believes that you could get emotionally hurt. As a result, it fires this 'fight or flight' response to warn you about the possible danger.

This kind of response does not serve us very well because it restricts us from doing things that would make us happy. It prevents us from going out and meeting interesting people who can potentially become our friends.

So why does the Amygdala perceives the social situations as a danger? Well, it has a lot to do with your own negative beliefs. You will read more about this in the next part.

The Takeaway

- The Amygdala is a small structure of the brain that affects emotion.
- To socially anxious people, the Amygdala perceives social situations as a threat and therefore triggers the stress response to warn you about the potential danger.

PART TWO
THE DEEP UNDERLYING PROBLEM

"Everything we hear is an opinion, not a fact. Everything we see is a perspective, not the truth."

MARCUS AURELIUS

"If you change the way you look at things, the things you look at change."

WAYNE DYER

FIVE
YOUR LIMITING BELIEFS

> I've had a lot of worries in my life, most of which never happened.
>
> MARK TWAIN

HAVE YOU EVER ASKED YOURSELF, "Why do I get anxious in front of other people? Why do I experience these anxiety symptoms?"

As we discussed in the previous chapter, the real reason why you have physical symptoms such as blushing or excessive sweating is that your brain perceives the social situation as a threat or a danger. As a result, it tries to protect you by activating the survival mechanism and showing the signals to urge you to either fight or flee.

So why does your subconscious mind detect social

situations as a danger? And what if you could change it?

If amygdala doesn't perceive social situations as a danger anymore, what would happen?

Well, the answer is quite simple: you will no longer experience the social anxiety symptoms. Instead, you will feel relaxed in the social situations.

Is this even possible? Changing how the brain reacts to certain types of situations? You may ask.

Let me tell you a good news: it is absolutely possible. You can change how your subconscious mind works and how Amygdala reacts to social situations.

In order to do this, you will have to change your deep, negative, limiting beliefs.

As Wayne Dyer said, you have to change your perspectives so that things would make better sense to you.

Of course, it's easier said than done. However, if you learn the right way to identify these beliefs and challenge them, you can condition your mind to replace these negative limiting beliefs with positive ones, and the Amygdala would start to react to social situations differently.

About limiting beliefs

Let's first take a look at what these limiting beliefs look like. Limiting beliefs can appear in any form and can be entrenched and resistant to logic or evidence to the contrary.

If you are a person suffering from social anxiety, I'm sure that you will find these statements very familiar.

Limiting beliefs about yourself:

- I'm too ugly, short, fat, deformed, weird...etc. No one would want to be friends with someone like me.
- I'm not good enough.
- I have to be perfect in order to be loved or accepted.
- I always say or do stupid things in front of people. I'm going to embarrass myself.
- I can't make friends because I'm a person with severe social anxiety.
- I can't make friends because of my race.
- I can't make friends because of my age.
- I can't make friends because of my sexuality.

- None of my interests are appealing to other people. People will think that I'm a boring person.

Limiting beliefs related to the people in the social situations:

- No one here is the type of person I'd like to hang out with.
- People here are not friendly.
- People here always talk bad behind my back.
- People here are too busy to make new friends.

Limiting beliefs related to the action of socializing itself:

- People will think I'm pathetic and desperate if I try to make friends with them.
- I can't go to a social event alone like a loser with no friends.
- I can't start conversations with strangers because I don't want to look like a creep.

These are all common limiting beliefs that become an obstacle to your successful social life.

It is important for you to understand that the one and only thing standing in your way are your own thoughts. Like I said, the real problem is not the anxiety, the deeper underlying problem is that your subconscious mind perceives danger in the social situations. You need your mind to believe that you're safe in the social settings by changing your limiting beliefs.

We will talk about how to deal with your negative thoughts in more details in the next part.

The Takeaway

- You can change how Amygdala reacts to social situations by changing your limiting beliefs.
- Limiting beliefs may be about yourself, the people around you, or the act of socializing itself.

SIX
LEARN TO ACCEPT YOURSELF

> Accept yourself, love yourself, and keep moving forward.
>
> ROY BENNETT

> No amount of self-improvement can make up for any lack of self-acceptance.
>
> ROBERT HOLDEN

THOSE WITH ANXIETY often find it difficult to accept oneself. However, self-acceptance plays an important role in panic and anxiety recovery. The reason is very simple. If you can't accept yourself, it is difficult to believe others will be able to accept you too.

So, what exactly is self-acceptance?

Self-acceptance is defined as the acceptance of oneself despite any existing deficiencies. It means being completely okay with who you are at this moment in time.

Self-acceptance involves self-understanding, as well as a subjective yet realistic awareness of strengths and weaknesses.

Self-acceptance doesn't mean you are giving up and accepting that you will never change. On the contrary, self-acceptance is the main pre-requisite for change. What you can't change – you have to accept first. When you accept it, you release the anxiety about it and this will allow you to free up your energy in order to tackle the challenges. It is what enables you to make the changes needed to become who you want to be.

Tips for Self-Acceptance

Know who you are:

Do you think you know who you are? What are your values? What is important to you in your life? What are your principles? What are you good at doing? What are your strengths and weaknesses? Write them down. It helps you to know yourself even better.

Understand that it is ok to be you:

When you look into a mirror, what do you think? Do you start thinking about all the points you don't like?
I'm too fat...
I don't like my nose...
I look tired...
Now I want you to do an exercise with me. Find a comfortable chair to sit in quietly for a moment. You can play some natural sounds such as beach or forest if you want. Pay attention to your body, your arms, legs, and head. Next, focus on your mind, your thoughts, feelings, and sensation.

Once you start feeling an inner calm, let a smile creep across your face and tell yourself:

"This is me and I'm completely ok with that."

Then, I want you to look into the mirror and try to stop any thoughts to judge yourself right there. Try to appreciate anything you can find for yourself. Once you have done that, tell yourself with a smile: "I am not perfect, but I accept myself completely."

It may be difficult to believe in yourself when you just start practicing, but as you keep repeating this exercise, you will soon be able to truly feel the acceptance and feel a sense of relief.

Understand that you are not your anxiety:

You have to realize that your anxiety does not define who you are. There is absolutely no reason not to accept yourself because of the label of being an anxious person that you think you have to wear. It's time for you to start to embrace the fact, rather than using it as an excuse to subconsciously undermine your feelings of self-worth.

Don't 'should' yourself:

The path towards self-acceptance is also about learning not to use statements that are too rigid. Lines such as "I shouldn't feel and act like this" and "I should be able to talk to people without being anxious" do not leave any room for compromises and would put you under too much pressure. If you always give yourself limitations, especially with how you feel, you won't be able to fully accept who you are.

Don't fall into the comparison trap:

It is normal to feel bad if you compare yourself unfavorably to others. You will always find people who are more attractive, make more money, have more accomplishments or simply have more likes on Facebook. However, these negative social comparisons do not help you to accept yourself. Instead, they can cause you to experience greater stress and anxiety.

Try not to compare yourself to others. Also, don't measure yourself to society's standards. Focus on yourself. Focus on your goal and your improvement. This can both motivate you and increase your self-esteem. Everyone is unique and you should find what makes you a great person. As Jennie Finch said: *"Try not to get lost in comparing yourself to others. Discover your gifts and let them shine!"*

The Takeaway

- Self Acceptance is defined as the acceptance of oneself despite any existing deficiencies.
- Self-acceptance is very important for anxiety recovery.
- You should get to know yourself better by

writing down your values, principles, strength, and weakness.
- It helps to do the self-acceptance exercise often and tell yourself that it is ok to be who you are.
- Your anxiety does not define who you are.
- It is helpful to learn not to use statements that are too rigid.
- It is not helpful to compare yourself unfavorably to other people.

SEVEN
INCREASE SELF-CONFIDENCE AND SELF-ESTEEM TO BEAT SOCIAL ANXIETY

> Low self-confidence isn't a life sentence. Self-confidence can be learned, practiced, and mastered - just like any other skill. Once you master it, everything in your life will change for the better.
>
> BARRIE DAVENPORT

Typically, people with a social anxiety disorder also suffer from low self-esteem. They hold themselves back and avoid situations in life. They avoid social situations because they fear being criticized and rejected by others.

Let's first talk about why building high self-esteem is so important by looking at the benefits of high self-esteem.

People with high self-esteem...

Trust themselves for decision making and don't seek validation of others:

If you have self-trust, then you can believe in your decisions instead of eagerly trying to get validation and attention from other people.

Feel more deserving of good things in life:

Most people who have low self-esteem tend to self-sabotage and feel that they don't deserve to be loved or to own good things. This is not a problem for those who have high self-esteem.

Are more attractive in any relationship:

People prefer spending their time with positive, self-confident people. People with high self-esteem are appreciated in any kind of relationships.

Have a simpler and happier life:

When you are self-confident, things simply become easier. You won't beat yourself up over simple mistakes or over not reaching a perfect standard.

WHAT ABOUT PEOPLE with low self-esteem?
Well, here's a list of behaviors and thoughts people with low self-esteem generally have:
People with low self-esteem...

- Are very self-conscious.
- Are often perfectionists because they are afraid of making mistakes or disappointing others.
- Are reluctant to make decisions because they are afraid of making the wrong one.
- Are overly sensitive to criticism.
- Constantly seek approval and acceptance from others.
- Don't believe in their abilities and skills.
- Don't trust their own opinion.
- Feel that they're not good enough.
- Feel that they do not deserve the good things in life.
- Have an intense fear of failure so they

won't try new things. Some of them would procrastinate taking actions.

Do you recognize any of these traits in yourself?

If you do, realize that it is not the end of the world. You can still learn and practice to develop self-esteem.

So how do you improve your self-esteem in a practical way?

Try these simple techniques to become more confident:

Sit up straight:

Research suggests that when we exercise proper posture, we tend to have a little more self-esteem. Recent findings also show that improving posture can improve the brain's function, such as your mood and memory levels.

Dress for success:

The old advice of dressing for the job you want comes in handy here. If you look the part, you will have the confidence to act the part.

Speak clearly and concisely:

Thinking before you speak and saying exactly what you mean will open doors for you.

Organize yourself and your space:

Just knowing where everything is, gives you the confidence that you can carry out a task with ease. Besides, looking for things before starting a project is an exhausting waste of time.

Stand up for yourself:

It's important to be assertive – no matter how hard it might seem. If you believe in yourself, you should have no problem advocating for yourself when your ethics are on trial. Assert yourself and let other people know what you have in mind. Express how you feel, but be ready for opposing views. Remember that not everyone is going to agree with you all the time and it is completely fine if others hold a different opinion.

Replace the perfectionism:

Perfectionism can paralyze you from taking action because you are so afraid of not living up to some standard. As a result, you procrastinate and you do not get the results you want. This will make your self-esteem sink. Instead of aiming for perfection, aim for "good enough".

Practice daily affirmations:

Making daily affirmations is one of the simplest, least time-consuming ways to boost your confidence. Pick a phrase that really hits home for you and your goals. You can use quotes from people that inspire you or do something generic such as "I am confident and strong. I am capable of dealing with whatever comes my way" or "I can solve problems. No challenge is too large for me to handle."

Surround yourself with confident and supportive people:

Choose to spend less time with people who are nervous, perfectionists or unsupportive of your goals. Instead, spend more time with positive, uplifting people. People who are confident exude their confidence, and it is an energy that can be felt. Just being around people who believe in themselves is contagious.

. . .

In the next part, you will find effective solutions that will help you overcome your social anxiety.

The Takeaway

- People with high self-esteem trust themselves for decision making and don't seek validation of others. They also feel more deserving of good things in life, are more attractive and have a happier life.
- People with low self-esteem are often very self-conscious, sensitive to criticism, and afraid of making decisions because of their fear of failure. They also think that they are not good enough and often seek validation of others.
- Techniques to become more confident include: maintaining good posture and wearing suitable clothes, being organized, being assertive...etc. Positive affirmations and confident, supportive people are also helpful for you to build your self-confidence.

PART THREE

4 STEPS TO OVERCOME SOCIAL ANXIETY

EIGHT
CHANGE THE STORIES YOU TELL YOURSELF

> If you think you can do a thing or think you can't do a thing, you're right.
>
> HENRY FORD

WE ALL HAVE this little voice that tells us stories that might not be helpful for us. In the social situations, these thoughts often go like:

–What I have to say isn't good enough. No one will be interested.

–He or she will think I'm boring, stupid, unattractive, or socially inept.

–They can tell I'm anxious and will think I'm either weird or weak.

–What if I get rejected?

–I might embarrass myself.
–I might say something stupid.

THESE UNHELPFUL THOUGHTS lead to feelings of discomfort and bring forth much bigger issues. They drain you of energy and keep you from being in the present moment. The more you give in to your negative thoughts, the stronger they become. The negativity can also affect your personal relationships, causing you to feel hurt or act defensively.

In chapter 5, we already discussed some common limiting beliefs that might stand in your way. In this chapter, you can further follow 3 steps to identify, challenge, and change your negative thoughts.

1. Identify Your Negative Thoughts Patterns

The first step to tackle unhelpful negative thoughts is to understand them.

These are some common types of unhelpful automatic thoughts.

Predicting the Future

When you're socially anxious or shy, you may spend a great deal of time pondering about your future. You may also make predictions on the things that might go wrong, instead of letting things unfold naturally. In the end, you often realize that your predictions are unreliable and you only wasted energy and time thinking relentlessly about negative situations that never occur.

Predicting too much about the future can make you unreasonably upset and worried. For example, you may assume that you'll do something to gain the attention of everyone or that you will be ostracized and rejected. These negative thoughts can make you feel anxious long before you even do something in a social setting.

All or Nothing Logic

Do you see things in such a way that there are only two possible outcomes? If facing a challenge is all about winning or losing, you're going to miss out on a lot of things. What's worse, you may end up setting impossibly high standards for yourself. This increases your chances of getting disappointed since failing to reach those standards is more likely.

By relying on an all-or-nothing logic, you could end up believing that you're a failure. What you would actually fail in though, is the practice of appreciating what's in between. Seeing the world as merely black and white causes you to overlook the lessons you gain from every challenge – regardless of whether you manage to exceed expectations.

Mind Reading

It's about making assumptions regarding what other people think of you without any actual evidence to support such assumptions. As we discussed in the previous chapter, you may readily assume that other people think that you are stupid or ugly. Because of your negative assumptions, you reduce your own self-esteem and you end up ruining your mood.

Personalization

Arguably among the most self-destructive thinking styles, personalization is all about taking the blame in all situations. Even in things that are yet to happen, a person who follows this line thinking will already assume responsibility if ever things do go south. What's even more concerning is the sheer willingness to take the blame, regardless of whether other people should be called out for their shortcomings.

Taking Things Personally

People who are shy or socially anxious tend to take things personally. This is because they quickly become emotionally vulnerable. Oftentimes, they make assumptions and draw conclusions without really thinking things through.

For example, they might think that they're being ignored when actually the people they are talking to are just busy. They may also think that they are being laughed at or ridiculed by others. They generally assume that everything is about them.

Overgeneralizing

People who overgeneralize tend to make assumptions based on isolated incidents. In their minds, the patterns are all the same.

For instance, they may lose the courage to audition for another play if their previous audition went bad. They may think that if they try again, it'll just be another failure. Likewise, if someone hurt them deeply, they'll assume outright that everyone else would do the same.

Self-Minimization

Many social anxiety sufferers put down themselves by minimizing the significance and weight of their own accomplishments. This way of thinking is usually accompanied by a tendency to overly praise and emphasize other people's qualities and triumphs. As to be expected, this will greatly affect both confidence and self-esteem.

I'll have to point out that this way of thinking doesn't always manifest in the most obvious ways. If you often claim that the praises you're getting are merely a result of people being polite, well, you might actually be using self-minimization. Likewise, if you usually find yourself saying that luck brought you success, you might have to reevaluate your views.

What If Statements

What if statements such as "What if I make a mistake and humiliate myself?" and "What if I get rejected?" make you fear or dread situations before they even start. Although these thoughts would be helpful if the next step is to come up with ways to prevent the worst outcomes, they're not typically followed by that kind of action.

In most cases, what if statements end up blowing

things out of proportion, creating feelings of doubt and even hopelessness. With that, the anxiousness will only worsen as the endeavor nears. Sometimes, things become too much to bear, making a person more likely to back out and miss an opportunity.

Thinking with Emotions

This simply refers to using only your emotions to evaluate things. An example of this would be avoiding a person just because you don't feel good about him. Likewise, thinking with your emotions will make you believe that things won't go your way because you feel that they won't – dismissing outright whatever proof you encounter that challenges that view, no matter how irrefutable it supposedly is.

Just to be clear, this isn't the same as what people mostly refer to as gut feeling. Intuition is at the core of every gut feeling, meaning that both emotion and logic are involved – the difference between this and proper thinking lies in the presence of conscious awareness. It could be said that whenever you have a gut feeling, you've already processed information automatically.

Focusing on the Negatives

People generally tend to ignore the brighter side of things. Because of this, they prevent themselves from feeling good. They also lower their self-confidence. For example, even though you have a lot of friends who like you, you may focus on a single person who dislikes you. Likewise, you may think of all the negative aspects of social situations while completely ignoring the positives.

Labelling

This is mainly about assigning unkind labels to yourself, which ruins your self-confidence and mood. It may also cause you to have feelings of hopelessness. Examples of labeling are telling yourself that you're stupid, unlovable, useless, ugly, boring, or a failure.

2. Challenge Your Unhelpful Thoughts

Whenever you find yourself harboring unhelpful thoughts, you should immediately act to prevent things from worsening. Ask yourself certain questions to verify the truthfulness behind the negativity.

For example, whenever you end up saying that

you're a failure, ask yourself if there is evidence to that particular claim.

What makes you think that you're a failure? If you made mistakes or were clumsy during a presentation, you might believe that you are a failure – after all, you made a fool of yourself in front of clients and embarrassed your bosses.

However, is this really true? Not doing very well during one presentation does not make you a failure. Recall your previous presentations. How did you do in those times? Were your clients and bosses impressed? Were you proud of yourself for delivering an excellent slideshow and for doing thorough research?

Perhaps, you were distracted during this recent presentation, and that's why everything did not go the way you planned. Perhaps, you had to do something more important the previous night, such as stay with your spouse in the hospital during his or her surgery. Even then, not every part of your presentation was a failure. Certainly, there were areas where you made some good points.

By asking yourself questions to verify the truthfulness of your negative assumptions and providing reasonable answers, you'll eventually come to the conclusion that you're not a failure. Your performance may have been subpar today, but that does not mean that you will perform poorly in the future.

3. Replace Negative Thoughts with Positive Thoughts

Once you have become more aware of your negative thought patterns and have challenged the thoughts, you are ready to replace negative thoughts with more realistic and positive thoughts. These positive thoughts will help you effectively face your day-to-day situations.

Avoid using negative language:

Words such as "won't", "can't", "always", and "never" really don't help you think more positively. Therefore, you should consciously make an effort to replace these words with words such as "will" and "can". Start by observing your thoughts and when you notice you use this language, remind yourself in the moment to use more positive or balanced language.

When you're in a negative situation, find what's good or helpful:

Think of negative thought replacement as comforting an upset child who just lost a game. What would you say to him? Maybe it would be something like: "Of course you're not a loser. You might not have won this game, but you played well. Remember how you scored last time? Besides, we can practice more and think about how you can win next time."

Imagine that your mind is a little child or a good friend. Whenever you notice a negative thought popping up in your mind, try to comfort this child or friend with a more empowering and positive thought.

For example, if you've failed in doing something, then negative thoughts may start to cloud your whole mind of this situation. However, you can always replace the thoughts by asking better questions, such as:

•What's one good thing about this situation?

•What's one thing I can learn from this?

•What's something I can do next time to have a better outcome?

I've included some useful positive statements in the Appendix for you. Try to replace your negative thoughts with these positive thoughts as often as possible. You will be surprised to start seeing a positive change in your life soon.

*See Appendix: Useful Positive Statements for Different Situations

The Takeaway

- You can free yourself from anxiety by having new perspectives and challenging unhelpful thoughts.
- The three steps to changing the unhelpful thoughts are: identify the negative thoughts, challenge the negative thoughts and replace the negative thoughts with positive ones.

NINE
STOP BEING OVERLY SELF-CONSCIOUS

> Care about what other people think and you will always be their prisoner.
>
> LAO TZU

Do you ever get that feeling that people are constantly judging you and looking at you?

As a matter of fact, social anxiety makes us worry excessively about how we're acting around others. We have a feeling that we're under a microscope and everybody is judging us. We stress over what we say, what we look like, and how we move. We're obsessed with how people perceive us.

"Do I look funny? Do I look nervous? Why is everybody looking at me?" Consequently, it is difficult for us to concentrate on living in the present moment and appreciate life.

It's really common to feel self-conscious when someone is looking at you. But as the novelist and teacher David Foster Wallace said: You'll worry less about what people think about you when you realize how seldom they do.

How to stop thinking that everyone is looking at me?

People with social anxiety constantly try to predict what will happen and read other people's mind. But as humans, we have no way to read someone else's mind.

The most important thing you have to realize is that people don't look at you as much as you think. Why?

Well, because most people have their own issues to think and worry about. Most people are preoccupied with their own thoughts, so they don't really pay that much attention to you.

A simple technique to try when you get this feeling that everyone is looking at you or judging you is to simply stop your thoughts and look around you.

Are they really paying attention to you? Or are they more lost in their own worlds?

As you do this, you will find that most people are just not paying that much attention to others.

This realization and reminder can help you to set yourself free from being too self-conscious and help you feel better.

Another way to think about this is to realize that your opinion about yourself is the only one that matters. If you think about it, you are not born to please everybody. You can live your life the way you want to be and stop seeking for people's approval, especially those who you do not even know.

The Takeaway

- People with social anxiety constantly try to read other's mind. However, there's no way to really know what others are thinking.
- When you feel self-conscious, it helps to stop your thoughts and observe the people around you. You will be surprised to find that not many people are paying that much attention to you because they are busy dealing with their own thoughts.

TEN
LEARN TO CONTROL YOUR BREATHING

Do you remember those short little breaths when you get nervous? These breaths actually cause you to be more anxious than you actually may be. Therefore, it is important to learn the basic relaxation techniques and practice them in the social events when you start to panic.

Anxiety typically causes poor breathing habits because it stimulates the autonomic nervous system and interferes with the normal breathing pattern.

To be specific, those with social anxiety generally suffer from shallow breathing or breathing in too quickly, over-breathing or breathing in more air due to the feeling of not getting sufficient amounts, and monitored breathing or overthinking about breathing.

Note that poor breathing habits can result in bigger problems, including hyperventilation. To start breathing better, you need to practice the following techniques:

Carbon Dioxide Rebreathing

Hyperventilation can make you feel as if you're not getting sufficient oxygen, when in fact, you are getting more oxygen than necessary. What's worse though, is that it causes your carbon dioxide levels to drop, which in turn will worsen the anxiety attack. Whenever you notice hyperventilation kicking in, you should cup your hand over your mouth and start to breathe slowly.

Deep Breathing

Deep breathing can soothe your body and help you relax. To do it, just sit in a chair, put your arms on the armrests, and straighten your back. Take a deep and slow breath. Inhale through your nose for five to six seconds, hold your breath in for a short while, and exhale through your mouth for about seven seconds. Do this ten times in a row.

Inhale-Hold-Exhale (Advanced)

This technique is basically a combination of carbon dioxide rebreathing and deep breathing. It can help you calm down faster. To begin, you have to sit down in a chair and keep yourself comfortable. Straighten your back and refrain from slouching. Monitor your heartbeat as you take ten breath cycles. For every cycle, you need to inhale for five heartbeats, hold your breath for seven heartbeats, and exhale for nine heartbeats. See to it that you inhale through your stomach and then your chest.

REMINDER: If you've been diagnosed with heart ailments, it's best to consult a physician before trying any breathing exercises. While there may be benefits to controlling the way you breathe, it may put additional strain on your heart – increasing the chances that your condition would worsen, even possibly causing a bigger health problem.

The Takeaway

- Breathing exercises are particularly effective in reducing anxiety.
- Effective exercises include Carbon Dioxide Rebreathing, Deep Breathing, and Inhale-Hold-Exhale techniques.

ELEVEN
PUT YOURSELF OUT THERE
THE EXPOSURE THERAPY

> If you want to conquer fear, don't sit home and think about it. Go out and get busy.
>
> DALE CARNEGIE

> If you always do what you've always done, you'll always get what you've always got.
>
> STEVEN HAYES

Now that you learned how to change your negative thoughts, stop being so self-conscious and control your breathing, it is time for you to put yourself out there. But first, let us talk about why avoidance doesn't work.

Why avoidance only makes it worse

People who are socially anxious tend to avoid social situations that stress them out. However, if a person does not confront the feared situation, and instead avoids it, the fear will be maintained.

Let's explain this phenomenon by looking at a term called negative reinforcement. In short, negative reinforcement means that a behavior is strengthened by removing or avoiding an unpleasant outcome. In the context of social anxiety, the behavior of avoidance serves to remove an unwanted or unpleasant consequence - in this case, anxiety symptoms. As a result, it leads to an increase of that behavior.

Let me give you another example of how negative reinforcement works. When you get inside your car and forget to put your seatbelt on, your alarm will go off to remind you to put it on. The beeping of the alarm is annoying, and the only way to make it stop is to put on your seatbelt. In other words, by putting on your seatbelt, you avoid the unpleasant noise of the alarm.

Let's now come back to the case of social anxiety. By avoiding the social situations, you no longer have to fight for the unpleasant anxiety symptoms. Your brain learns that it is an effective coping strategy and tells you that you should keep doing it.

Here is a concrete example in the context of social

anxiety to further explain this concept. Suppose Jason is a person who has social anxiety. He receives an invitation to a school party and starts to feel anxious about this event. Next, the limiting beliefs will start to kick in. He may begin to think, "I will probably say something stupid and people will make fun of me." With these thoughts, Jason feels extremely uncomfortable. However, if he decides to not attend the party in order to avoid the unpleasant feelings, his anxiety level will decrease right away.

Since his anxiety decreased by avoiding the anxiety-provoking situation, this behavior (avoidance) is negatively reinforced by the removal of these negative feelings.

Now his brain has learned that avoidance is a highly effective strategy to reduce or even eliminate the uncomfortable feelings. Thus, if Jason receives another invitation next time, he is likely to cope with the situation with the method that worked well before.

Although in the short-term this strategy may seem effective to reduce the anxiety, in the long-term it only interferes with the person's ability to overcome fear.

Think about it, every time you try to reach a goal and yet allow fear to overcome you, you practice avoidance and negatively reinforce the behavior. You should realize that the more often you avoid situations that make you socially anxious, the more likely you'll avoid social situations in the future. The result? Well, the person who avoids social situations regularly will remain socially isolated and unable to enjoy the many benefits of social relationships.

The Solution: The Exposure Therapy

So if the avoidance doesn't work, what should we do? Well, the only way is to get yourself out there. Exposure therapy involves facing social situations to reduce symptoms as well as to disrupt anxiety-related expectancies.

Although exposure therapy is usually conducted with the assistance of a therapist as part of a cognitive-behavioral treatment program, it is possible to be incorporated into your daily life.

How Exposure Therapy Works

Step 1: Develop a fear ladder

It is helpful to know what makes you socially anxious. Are you afraid of greeting your coworkers? Are you afraid of eating alone in a public area?

Spend some time observing your social anxiety and identifying the social situations that cause you anxiety.

When you understand what triggers your anxiety, you can then build a fear ladder. A fear ladder is an ordered list of your anxiety that begins with the least fearful situation to the most fearful one.

Below is a list of common types of feared social situations.

- Talking to co-workers
- Dealing with conflict
- Eating and drinking in front of others
- Using public bathrooms
- Small talk
- Meeting new people
- Speaking in a meeting
- Going to a party
- Public speaking
- Interacting with unfamiliar people
- Being the center of attention
- Speaking to authority figures

You should customize this list by adding or crossing out some situations. Then, on a scale of 10 with 10 being the scariest, rate each situation.

After you rate all the situations, you can now make an ordered list. Here is an example of a fear ladder:

- 1/10 - Using public bathrooms

- 2/10 - Eating in front of others
- 3/10 - Talking to coworkers
- 7/10 - Going to a party
- 8/10 - Meeting new people

This list differs from person to person, so make sure that you make a list that is really tailored to your own situation.

Step 2: Tackle the social anxiety by climbing the fear ladder

Once you have your fear ladder, you can now start facing your fears by putting yourself in these situations. Use the bottom-up approach. Start with the least scary situation. Repeat it until you feel less anxious doing it.

When you are able to enter the situation without feeling anxious, move to the next level of the ladder.

While you are climbing the fear ladder, it is very important to not avoid the situations. Also, never expect to have massive improvements right away. It is normal that you feel uncomfortable at first. After all, it is a very challenging exercise and it takes time and patience.

When you feel your fear, you just have to push yourself through that uncomfortable feeling. Keep doing it day by day. Before you know it you can push a little more. Soon you will feel your fear level declines and you feel more confident in each social situation.

The Takeaway

- People with social anxiety tend to avoid situations that make them anxious. However, avoidance is a form of negative reinforcement and would only make problems worse.
- Exposure therapy is a treatment that involves facing social situations to reduce symptoms as well as to disrupt anxiety-related expectancies.
- While using exposure therapy, start from the easier tasks and move to a harder task once you become comfortable with your current one.

PART FOUR
LIFESTYLE CHANGES TO REDUCE ANXIETY

"Success is the sum of small efforts, repeated day in and day out."

ROBERT COLLIER

TWELVE
DIET & EXERCISES

To REDUCE your anxiety levels and improve your well-being, you can start with modifying your lifestyle. Make changes in your diet and exercise routine. Choose healthier alternatives as much as possible.

Cutting Off Your Caffeine

For starters, you can avoid or limit your intake of caffeine. Coffee, tea, energy drinks, and cola all act as stimulants. This means they work on your central nervous system, affecting several hormones and chemicals.

You're probably familiar with adrenaline. It's the hormone that's most often brought up whenever the body's fight or flight response is being discussed. It's capable of raising your heart rate and blood pressure. It also opens up air passages to improve oxygen distribution. While those may seem advantageous, don't forget that anxiety basically does the same thing to your system. So, imagine what would happen if ever your anxiety kicks in while you still have caffeine in your bloodstream. I've experienced that firsthand and I know how unpleasant it can be.

Low adenosine levels make adrenaline secretion possible. Whenever there's an abundance of adenosine, you begin to feel tired and sluggish. Falling asleep at night is actually due to the chemical reaching its peak amount. As you'd expect, it's at its lowest when you wake up in the morning. In the presence of caffeine though, the fatigue-signaling chemical fails to reach the brain. The stimulant and psychoactive drug is structured similarly to adenosine, meaning the former literally blocks the latter from interacting with brain receptors.

Ideally, you should cut out caffeine from your diet entirely. If you've been drinking coffee and other similar beverages for so long though, you might need to do things gradually. The stimulant affects dopamine as well, temporarily keeping it at high amounts in the brain – that's why it tends to be addictive. Slowly reduce the amount of caffeine you take in daily. Eventually, you'll no longer crave for it even in minimal amounts.

Get Your Muscles Moving

You should also be physically active. Make exercising a priority. You have to sweat for at least thirty minutes daily. If you've always been sedentary, you can start with low-intensity exercises to minimize the risk of injury. Examples of low-intensity exercises include brisk walk or jog.

As time passes by and as your body gets used to working out, you should increase the intensity of your exercises. You can start lifting weights and pairing cardio with strength training routines. If working out at the gym doesn't appeal to you, try other forms of exercises such as yoga and Pilates. Engaging in sports such as basketball, volleyball, swimming, and tennis is also a good option.

Aside from exercising, you should make an effort to stay physically active at work. For example, instead of taking the elevator to reach your floor, you can opt for the stairs. Instead of parking closer to your office building, you should park a little bit farther away so that you have to walk more. You can also decide to walk home rather than drive or take a cab.

On Better Dietary Choices

Regarding your diet, you should take more omega-3 fatty acids. They support brain health and raise mood levels, helping you deal with anxiety better. You can get omega-3 fatty acids from fatty fish, such as salmon, herring, mackerel, anchovies, and sardines. You can also get them from seaweed, flaxseeds, and walnuts.

Avoid Alcohol and Nicotine

As much as possible, refrain from drinking alcoholic beverages. If you have to drink during social occasions, make sure that you only do so in moderation. Some people tend to drink more alcohol to calm their nerves, but you have to know that this practice is rather misguided. If you drink more alcohol, you only increase your risk of having an anxiety attack later on.

Alcohol is known to lower serotonin levels. As you might have heard, serotonin is another brain chemical that gives feelings of happiness. Whenever your supply of serotonin gets too low, you'll become anxious and even feel depressed. Given what you're trying to overcome, it's definitely counterproductive to consume something that's only going to worsen your fears and worries later on.

Likewise, you should refrain from smoking. A lot of

people have this misconception that smoking can help calm their nerves. Well, smoking will not do you any good. It will only cause your anxiety levels to go up – especially since it's no longer as widely accepted as it used to be. Besides, the vice can have a significant effect on your looks in the long run. People tend to notice dry skin and yellow teeth rather quickly.

Also, keep in mind that nicotine doesn't merely function as a sedative. As a matter of fact, when you smoke, your adrenal glands get stimulated and adrenaline gets released. So, why is it that many associate smoking with calm? Aside from giving you a quick burst of adrenaline, nicotine triggers dopamine secretion – and as you've learned, that chemical creates a feeling of happiness. Still, it's best to remember that the effect is temporary.

Get Enough Quality Sleep

It is important for you to get adequate amounts of rest and sleep. Don't ever think that sleep is only for the weak. In fact, sleep is necessary for you to function at your best. If you lack sleep, you also become more prone to anxiety. After all, you have to be well rested to stay calm during social situations. To get better sleep, you should go to bed and wake up at the same time every day and use the hour before bed for quiet time.

The Takeaway

- If you're really serious about beating social anxiety, you need to make several important changes in your life.
- Eating right, avoiding caffeine, getting enough rest, staying physically active, and putting an end to your vices are just some of the things you'll need to do.

THIRTEEN
MINDFULNESS

Mindfulness is another effective tool suited for the socially anxious. A lot of people become angry, frustrated, and upset with their condition, further worsening their anxiety.

So, instead of fighting your experiences by convincing yourself that you shouldn't feel how you feel, let yourself feel freely. When you acknowledge how you feel and let it be, you allow it to go away naturally. To make things easier, try these mindfulness techniques:

Finger Breathing

This will provide you with a visual object to focus on. It also gives you something to use your hands with. Begin by holding a hand in front of you, with your palm facing your direction. Use your index finger from your other hand to trace the outer length of your thumb as you inhale. Pause for a while and trace down the other side as you exhale. This counts as one breath. Do the same thing with your other fingers. Trace along as you count your breaths.

Your Five Senses

In this technique, you'll have to sit down and scan your surroundings. Now, among the things you see, choose five – it's best to go for those that you don't often pay attention to. Chipped paint, a cobweb, or even an ornament you've already forgotten about are just a few good examples. See these objects for what they are. Don't try to evaluate them in any way.

Once you're done, you'll have to take note of four things currently touching your skin. You can include almost anything such as the chair's armrest and the clothes you're wearing. After that, you must shift from the sense of touch to the sense of hearing. Observe three sounds. Again, there's no limit to what you may choose.

When you've spent enough time listening, you'll have to use your nose. Choose two smells and focus on them for a while. By the way, although you're free to pick any scent, it's best to go for those that seem new to you. At this point, the only thing left to do is to taste. Open your mouth and taste the air. Try to describe what it tastes like.

The Takeaway

- Mindfulness is a great way to help you overcome your anxiety.
- Begin by practicing the finger breathing and your five senses techniques.

PART FIVE
30-DAY CHALLENGE TO OVERCOME SOCIAL ANXIETY

"The journey of a thousand miles begins with a single step."

LAO TZU

FOURTEEN
BEFORE THE CHALLENGE

In this part of the book, you will be presented with a 30-day challenge wherein you will learn how to improve your life one day at a time. It's basically a form of exposure therapy that's also designed to gradually improve your confidence. Before you start though, you have to follow these steps:

Step 1: Start with Some Goal-Setting

What is your goal for embarking on this challenge? What do you want to achieve? Before you begin any great undertaking, it's important for you to determine your goals or objectives. In this case, your main goal is to overcome social anxiety. Of course, you can have other related goals, such as being able to make new friends, asking someone out on a date, doing well on a job interview, or having the courage to audition for a part in a play. Whatever your goals are, you have to lay them out. If you have read my book Mental Toughness, then you are familiar with the SMART goal-setting method. Just remember that a good goal should be Specific, Measurable, Attainable, Realistic and Timely.

Step 2: Make a Clear and Detailed Plan

Whether you'd choose to follow this 30-day challenge or decide to come up with your own, you'll need a detailed plan to increase your chances of succeeding in every daily task. You need to be sufficiently specific when listing the steps you'll have to take in completing a challenge. It would also help to have a backup plan just in case your first one suddenly becomes impossible to carry out.

Step 3: Do Affirmation and Positive Self-talk

It's crucial to condition your mind and body even before the challenge, and the best way to do this is to practice affirmation and positive self-talk.

Every day, recite good things about yourself. Keep yourself motivated and inspired by recalling your good qualities or attributes. The positive thoughts you feed your mind can do good things for your body. When both your mind and body are ready, you increase your capacity to succeed in the challenge.

Step 4: Prepare a Journal for Tracking Your Progress

Lastly, you need to have a physical record that you can look back on. You can use a journal or notebook to track your progress as you go through the challenge. After thirty days, you should read your entries and evaluate what you've accomplished so far. Seeing your past entries can help you determine how much growth you have achieved within this specific timeframe and how much more progress you can achieve in the future.

FIFTEEN

THE 30-DAY CHALLENGE

> Don't wait until everything is just right. It will never be perfect. There will always be challenges, obstacles, and less than perfect conditions. So what? Get started now. With each step you take, you will grow stronger and stronger, more and more skilled, more and more self-confident, and more and more successful.
>
> MARK VICTOR HANSEN

WHILE YOU ARE TAKING this 30-day challenge to overcome your social anxiety, I want you to be patient with yourself. If you simply cannot accomplish a task, then let it go and try it again the next day. Do not judge yourself or be too harsh on yourself. Remember, it takes time and patience.

Some challenges may appear silly or ridiculous to you, but they are designed for you to step out of your comfort zone. Therefore, I suggest that you practice them without questioning too much. You will be surprised how they can affect your self-esteem and social life.

You can start this challenge anytime, but just remember to take notes about how you feel every day and record your progress. It is important to celebrate your quick and small wins, too!

When you are mentally prepared, you can start this 30-day challenge!

The 30-Day Challenge

Day 1: Practice walking, sitting and standing with a proper posture. Keep your chin up, your shoulders back, and chest high. Don't rush when walking. Maintain grace as you move around.

Day 2: Continue maintaining proper posture throughout the day. This time though, you'll also have to pay attention to the people around you. Take note of the things that make each person unique.

Day 3: Smile at your officemates. If you're confident enough, you may even smile at those in the streets or in the subway. Try not to avoid eye contact. Remember that you'll still have to keep a proper posture as you do these things.

Day 4: Continue with what you've been doing so far. Regardless of how successful you've been up to this point, you need to become much more comfortable with your posture and try to smile at people around you.

Day 5: Recite your favorite movie lines or read your favorite poem out loud while relaxing in your room. This will prepare you for the coming tasks by making you a lot more comfortable with the sound of your own voice.

Day 6: Call up a company and inquire about their services. You'll have to keep the conversation going for as long as possible. So, it might be best to call a company that actually interests you.

Day 7: Call up an old friend or relative that you have not spoken to for a while. Chat about anything, but do your best to learn as much as possible about important life events that have recently transpired.

Day 8: It's finally time for some pleasantries. Greet early morning joggers in your neighborhood. Greet those in your office elevator as well. Practice your eye contact and smile. If you bought something, don't forget to thank the person behind the counter and start a small conversation if possible.

Day 9: Recall the number of people you've exchanged pleasantries within the previous day. Now, try to beat that number. If you're feeling rather confident, don't count those you've greeted or thanked the day before.

Day 10: It's time to increase the difficulty a bit. Strike up a conversation with an officemate you rarely get to work with. You don't have to talk about anything in particular, but aim to keep the conversation going for at least a minute.

Day 11: Approach a stranger and ask for the time. You can also walk up to any person on the street and ask for directions. This will prepare you for the things you'll have to do in the following days.

Day 12: Talk to random people in the shops. This will be a tough one, but try to engage in polite conversations whenever the opportunity arises. This should be easier where long lines are common, such as in supermarkets and coffee shops.

Day 13: Take a cab today. Have a pleasant conversation with the cab driver. Try to keep talking throughout the duration of the ride. If you're having a hard time thinking of a good topic, consider asking how his day went or where his previous stop was.

Day 14: You're already becoming more confident with how you move and talk, so it's time to take things further. Wear something nice with a bright color or bold outfit today. Talk to the people who compliment you about your look.

Day 15: Can you handle a potentially awkward situation? Just walk up to a stranger and tell him that he looks familiar. Then, ask him if he went to your old high school.

Day 16: Grab a book and head to your local coffee shop. Read your book for several hours. Strike up a conversation with the barista and other customers. Talk to at least three people.

Day 17: Do the same thing you did yesterday, but move to another coffee shop – particularly one that you haven't visited yet. Also, this time around, you'll have to talk with at least five people. If you have a hard time coming up with conversation ideas, compliment on their outfit or start by asking what time it is. Try not to stop there though. Try to be genuinely curious about what he or she is doing.

Day 18: Go to the diner by yourself and have conversations with the waitresses and staff. Make it your goal to chat with as many people as possible without asking the same things over and over.

Day 19: Sign up for a class, club or get a gym membership. This can be a yoga class, a guitar class, a painting class or anything you want to try out. It can be an activity that you have wanted to try for a long time. However, you shouldn't merely fill out forms and pay.

Make it a point to ask every relevant question you can come up with.

Day 20: Talk to at least three people in the class or gym you chose. It's going to be relatively easy, considering that you'll really have a lot of questions – and you'll be viewed as a newbie as well.

Day 21: You'll be doing the same task, but you need to widen your circle. Do your best to converse with at least five people this time in the class or at the gym. Introduce yourself and ask them how long they have been a member of the group. Once again, if you want a bit of a challenge, don't count those you've talked with the day before.

Day 22: Go out to lunch with a friend and get to know him or her better. You may also persuade him or her to hang out the entire day or at least for several hours – it'll be good practice given your greater confidence and improved communication skills.

Day 23: Ask a coworker you seldom speak with to go to lunch together today. Get to know him or her and schedule another lunch for next week.

Day 24: It's time to raise the stakes. Approach your boss and start a conversation. While it would be best to prepare an actual suggestion, it's perfectly fine to simply provide your views on certain things at work. If you are self-employed, sign up for a seminar related to your work and talk to the speaker after the event.

Day 25: Download the Meetup app and sign up for a meetup event that you are interested in tonight. You might want to talk yourself into not going at the last minute, but you will have to be strong and force yourself a bit. At the event, talk to three people and exchange ideas.

Day 26: Invite at least two people from work to have dinner or have a drink with you. To increase your chances of succeeding, come up with a good reason for inviting them. Also, it would be ideal to approach those known to be quite outgoing.

Day 27: Attend a party by yourself and introduce yourself to people. Make at least five new friends before the day ends. If you're raring for a bigger challenge, try to exchange contacts with your new acquaintances.

Day 28: Call three people you met from the previous meetings in the 30-day challenge and ask to meet for a second time.

Day 29: You have two options for this day. You could either attend another party or go to a meet-up. What's important is that you converse with a new set of people and further expose yourself to group settings.

Day 30: The final challenge is obviously the hardest. Go to a bar or club but stay sober. Engage in conversations with at least five people and try to get their contact information. Do your best to make new friends (get as many numbers as possible).

Feel free to consider this 30-day challenge as an example. However, if you wish to try the challenge as is, you may still have to tweak some tasks to suit your current situation. For example, if you're working as a freelance artist and you do not work in an office building, you can use alternatives. Instead of talking to your boss, you can pitch your ideas to a client. Instead of asking someone in your office for assistance, you can ask a neighbor for help on something. When the thirty days are up, begin creating a new set of challenges.

CONCLUSION

I hope this book was able to help you learn everything you need to know about social anxiety, from its basic definition to the steps you need to take to overcome the disorder.

Having social anxiety isn't easy. The disorder prevents you from living your life to the fullest. It keeps you from going out of the house to enjoy your beautiful surroundings. It robs you of the opportunity to maximize and showcase your skill sets. It even takes away your chances for building satisfying personal relationships by hindering your progress in romantic relationships and friendships. Likewise, it stops you from developing professional connections. In essence, it prevents you from functioning normally in society.

Nevertheless, social anxiety isn't untreatable. Through this book, you have learned about the ways and techniques that you can use to improve your condition. Little by little your anxiety levels will go down and you will find yourself becoming at ease during social situations. With consistent effort, you can go from joining small private gatherings to attending big social events. You'll transition from speaking only to a handful of close relatives and friends to addressing a large crowd.

You can train yourself to get used to social situations. You can also anticipate events and practice your actions. By familiarizing yourself with the appropriate techniques, you can make significant improvements, personally and professionally. Keep in mind though, that overcoming social anxiety entails doing a lifestyle overhaul as well. You'll need to modify your exercise routine and eating habits. The journey to wellness isn't short. It's a lifetime commitment. You need to do your best to overcome social anxiety every single day. Otherwise, you'll go back to square one and possibly lose everything you have worked so hard for.

If things get too difficult though, don't hesitate to ask for help. You may even reach out to medical professionals for advice regarding your condition. Never forget that you're not the only one suffering from the disorder, and there are lots of people who can and want to help you – and when you finally succeed in overcoming social anxiety, it'll be your turn to spread awareness and help others.

Thank you for reading this book and congratulations for reaching its final pages. I sincerely hope that you'll soon overcome social anxiety and begin living a happier, more satisfying life.

3. COMMUNICATION IN MARRIAGE

THE SECRET TO FIGHT LESS, LOVE MORE, AND CREATE THE HAPPY MARRIAGE YOU WANT

INTRODUCTION

Marriages are one of the most wonderful things to have in this world. If it works, it gives a lifetime of fulfillment for the two people involved. However, marriages are under siege for many reasons. More divorces are being filed over the years, and it doesn't tell the complete picture of how many marriages go down the drain every single day.

While there are many factors that play a role in a successful marriage, there is one element that should never be overlooked: communication. In fact, we have just devoted an entire book in showing exactly that.

Why Communication in Marriage Is Important?
1. Communication creates strong bonds
Building all levels of relationships require commu-

nication from all parties involved. It is no secret that couples that communicate well with each other have longer and happier marriages. On the flipside, couples that are barely able to connect with each other are less likely to keep their marriages afloat.

Constant communications help in developing stronger bonds. Couples learn more about each other, become better equipped in handling problems, and share their best life experiences when they constantly keep an open line of communication with one another.

2. Communication prevents misunderstandings, confusions, and wrong assumptions

Misunderstandings, confusions, and wrong assumptions are three of the most common reasons for conflicts in all levels of relationships. In the context of marriages, keeping these things unresolved may lead to all kinds of problems. Arguments can go out of hand, marital matters are taken out of context, and supposed non-issues become the trigger for major conflicts.

The best solution to prevent misunderstandings, confusions, and wrong assumptions is with healthy communication. You will be surprised on how many of these issues can be resolved if married couples know how to reach out to each other.

3. Communication keeps couples emotionally connected

Establishing an emotional connection with your spouse is crucial in establishing a foundation for a strong marriage. Conversely, maintaining an emotional connection with your spouse is important to ensure that it will last a lifetime.

It is no secret that constant and healthy communication is one ingredient that keeps couples emotionally invested with each other. Couples that maintain constant contact with each other create more happy memories, share more experiences together, and are happier with each other in general.

4. Communication helps in resolving marital conflicts

There are all kinds of things that are potential sources for marital conflicts (a section is specifically dedicated for this). While there are many ways to prevent and resolve conflicts in marriage, communication is one of the most powerful of them.

Aside from the fact that it can be used for correcting different issues, proper communication is also helpful in preventing these problems from surfacing in the first place. When couples are able to effectively talk out their concerns and problems, they are able to find solutions for them and prevent them from further compromising the relationship.

Who Is This Book For?

This book is created for couples everywhere. It doesn't matter what the age, number of years married, or the current status of the couple is. If you are a married couple, you can greatly benefit from improving communication and the benefits it brings to your relationship.

Whether you are trying to take your marriage to the next level or you are trying to mend a marriage that is on the rocks, developing communication between the couple would be extremely beneficial. So in essence, this book is created for every married couple out there.

This book is created for couples that are encountering problems. It is common for all couples to run into problems. Couples, healthy or otherwise, can run into all kinds of issues that may cause them to butt heads. However, for one reason or another, these problems can become the basis of the breakdown of the relationship.

There are a lot of marriages that end up in separation or divorce, and they are often caused by reasons that could have otherwise been prevented. One of our motivations in creating this book is to help couples save a troubled marriage. There are many tools to save a

INTRODUCTION

marriage, and one of the most powerful of them is communication.

This book is also created for married couples who are currently in a healthy relationship. Even if things are going great in your relationship, there are so many ways to further improve it. One of the best ways to keep marriages alive is to improve your communication. Constant communication is one of the best ways to get to know your partner better, reignite romance, and resolve issues that make problems in both short and long terms.

Aside from improving your communication as a couple, this book will also teach you effective techniques successful couples use to keep their marriage strong in spite of multiple adversities they face every day.

ONE
THE TRUTH ABOUT HAPPY MARRIAGES

> *The success of marriage comes not in finding the right person, but in their ability of both partners to adjust to the real person they inevitably realized they married.*
>
> JOHN FISCHER

PEOPLE ARE ENAMORED by the presence of happy marriages. After all, who doesn't want to be happily married? The surprising thing is that in spite of this strong desire, more couples are still heading towards disagreements, and in some cases leading to complete breakups.

A lot of people who are in relationships that are going south ask these questions.

What do these couples have that we don't? What are their secrets to staying happy and contented?

While there are many things that make marriages work, one of the most important elements found in successful relationships is healthy communication.

What makes marriages work?

Not all marriages last, but those that did have a secret or two that made things work for them. This is no single greatest element that makes marriages work. Rather, the success of a marriage is dependent on multiple factors that work hand in hand that keep couples together in spite of forces that can potentially tear them apart. Here are some of the things that make marriages work.

1. Mutual respect

Respect is a foundational element in any kind of interpersonal relationship. This is especially so when it comes to major relationships such as marriages. It is important that both husband and wife respect each other when it comes to all matters. Of course, respecting doesn't mean you have to agree with everything they say or do, but there is always a proper way to express your displeasure.

A constant showing of disrespect not only presents a red flag for the relationship, but it is also a sign that the person has personality issues. If you love your spouse, respect comes out naturally, even if you don't agree with each other all the time.

2. Knowing how to properly handle problems

One of the hallmark traits of healthy marriages is the ability to solve problems the right way. There are no marriages that don't run into their fair share of issues, but the way couples handle these issues is what separates functional marriages from dysfunctional ones.

When happily married couples are shown with problems, they sit down together and look for solutions in a calm manner. Both sides are heard before making decisions, especially important ones. They take into consideration the feelings of the other before making any choice. Lastly, a healthy marriage knows that their alliance is much bigger than any of the issues that they face.

3. Embracing of imperfections

There is no such thing as a perfect marriage. How the couple handles such imperfections is one of the things that define healthy marriages. Your partner will always have their fair share of flaws. It is up to you to accept these and never let them tear your marriage apart.

However, beyond acceptance, the person must still try to fix the flaws that they can correct. Also, both sides are accountable for telling their spouse what they are doing wrong. Of course, they should do this in a nice way, always in consideration of the other person's feelings.

4. The marriage is a priority

When you get married, you and your partner enter into a contract that you will stay together for each other no matter what. While separation and divorce is there as an option if all else fails, a functional married couple understands that they should make the marriage work at all costs.

To make sure the marriage works, both sides should make it a priority. Both sides should make the necessary steps to provide for the marriage, to give time to their partner, to resolve conflicts, and share life experiences together. When both you and your partner prioritize your marriage, everything else, from the children to the expenses, will fall into place.

5. A constant effort to make things work

It is certainly not easy to make marriages work. It takes time, effort, passion, compassion, and tons of patience to make a marriage work. With so many responsibilities and problems to face throughout your married life, it is paramount that both sides make the effort to make things work.

It's not going to work if it's only one side that's trying to solve problems, perform responsibilities, and show affection towards their partner. As early as in the courtship stage, romantic relationships are always a two-way street. This rings even truer once you get married. Make the effort to make things work, even if you get into each other's faces from time to time.

How to know that there's a problem in your marriage?

In any marriage, there would always be problems. They can come in all kinds of forms; some of them trivial, while others almost always put the marriage itself to the test. Some problems manifest right away, while others are more insidious, only surfacing when the damage to the marriage is already significant.

It is important that both you and your partner are able to identify when there is a problem in your marriage. Doing so will help both of you to resolve them before they end up costing you your marriage. Here are some signs that your marriage is having serious problems.

1. You fight more often and for the wrong reasons

Fighting is always a part of every kind of relationship. Even the best-maintained relationships have their share of arguments, and sometimes fighting is a good sign that both sides are willing to work out their differences. However, there comes a point when fighting is not healthy anymore.

When you are fighting too often, that is not a very good sign. This may mean that you are not communicating well, insisting on having your way instead of finding a common ground. You also fight about things that are not worth fighting about. A lot of unhealthy fights are triggered by unnecessary criticisms and bringing up past faults. If you and your partner are fighting like this, your marriage is very much on the rocks.

2. Both of you show increased disrespect for each other

One of the most important elements in a marriage is a mutual respect for one another. One of the most obvious signs that a relationship is going south is when the couple is losing respect for each other. Some disrespect their partners deliberately, while others show a lack of respect for them unconsciously thru some actions.

One or both starts to harbor resentment towards their partner, and they sometimes show it thru avoidance or aggression. Also, you are happier when your partner is not around and sometimes you shamefully show it to the world. Once disrespect takes over a marriage, it won't be long until its dissolution commences.

3. Intimacy is significantly reduced

In a marriage that is on the rocks, intimacy becomes significantly reduced. Most people think that loss of intimacy in marriage is defined by loss of sexual desire and passion, but it goes deeper than that. Loss of intimacy is evident in just about every interaction that you have.

The small things that you do when you are just

married, the sharing of affection, the sweet words, the simple shows of care that makes married life an enjoyable one, all start to fade. When you start feeling no emotion towards your partner, it is a major red flag for a marriage. It means that intimacy is fading, and you got to do something before it's too late.

4. Conversations are dominated by problems

One of the hallmarks of a failing marriage is that the couple refuses to talk to each other anymore. It is a sign that they can't stand each other and/or they feel that nothing worthwhile can be had when they talk. It is basically a telltale sign that the couple has given up on each other and that conversations only serve as an additional source of stress.

If conversations do exist, it is in the form that is far from being productive. Conversations between couples at odds with each other tend to be toxic, as they tend to focus on negative things such as their problems, the flaws of their partners, and the like. Plus, there seems to be an inability or unwillingness in the couple to solve such problems.

5. You can't trust each other

Trust is another foundational element in all marriages, and basically in all forms of interpersonal relationships, in general. After all, can you consider it a healthy marriage if you don't trust each other? There are many ways that a person can show that they don't trust someone.

Suspicion is a dominant theme in a couple that doesn't trust each other. Accusations of having affairs, questioning what they do when they are not together, and constant presumptions of lying are obvious signs of distrust. A couple that cannot trust each other is a sign of an unhealthy marriage.

What does great communication in marriage look like?

1. It is communication filled with empathy

Empathy is such an important component in any kind of relationship. No matter you're a newlywed or married for at least half a century, empathy plays an important role in successful marriages. A marriage with empathy is wherein both husband and wife make every effort to consider what's in the mind and heart of the other.

Being emphatic, opens doors to explanation and negotiation, allows forgiveness and tolerance to reign, and fosters acceptance and appreciation of your partner and what you have as a couple. Never forget to talk and listen to your partner with empathy. You can never go wrong with it.

2. Communication is constructive by nature

There are many ways to know if couples are communicating in a destructive manner.

First, there is excessive focusing on problems. Second, the couple refuses to listen to what the other person has to say. And third, there is outright disrespect in both verbal and nonverbal elements of the conversation. Healthy communications should be constructive by nature. It should aim to resolve conflicts, improve understanding, and be done in consideration of each person's feelings.

3. The couple aims to resolve conflicts

Conflicts would always be a part of every marriage. What separates healthy marriages from unhealthy marriages is the way they approach these conflicts.

This would be immediately apparent with the way that they talk.

Healthy marriages use communication as means for resolving conflicts that they place on an everyday basis. The couple aims to resolve their conflicts, not merely prove that they are right or their partner is wrong. They don't let their anger or personal biases affect their conversation. They use conversation to arrive at a resolution that satisfies both parties while keeping the relationship intact.

4. Both sides listen to each other and respect each side

A healthy communication is where both sides listen. Many failing relationships don't look at each other eye to eye when they talk, let alone take the time to hear what they say. Whether they are right or wrong, everyone deserves to be heard. It's a basic element of respect.

Once you start listening to your partner, it is easier to come up with a resolution that satisfies both sides. At the same time, it is a simple way to avoid further conflict. After all, no one wants to feel that their side is not being heard out.

5. Communication aims to build relationships, not break them

The end goal of healthy communication in marriages is to build relationships, not break them. It is never a good thing is your aim to talk to your partner is to put them down, to assert that your idea is always better than theirs. You should approach each moment of communication, no matter how mundane the subject or how contentious the situation, as a means to further improve your marriage. At the end of the day, staying together is more important than winning a debate or two.

The Takeaway

- Marriages work because of a combination of factors. The most successful couples respect each other at all times, solve problems together, and make their marriage a priority.
- There are different signs of a failing marriage. They fight for the wrong reasons, have utter disrespect for each other, and have lost intimacy and trust.
- Communication is an important element of successful marriages. The way a couple

communicates gives you an idea of the marriage's health.
- Healthy communication in marriage looks like this: it features empathy, both sides listen to each other, it is constructive by nature, and it nurtures the marriage.

THERE ARE many things that can prevent a couple from having great communication. One of the most common reasons why couples can't get along is because of the simple differences between male and female. In the next chapter, you will learn more about the communication differences between men and women.

TWO
THE COMMUNICATION DIFFERENCES BETWEEN MEN AND WOMEN

> *Ultimately, the bond of all companionship, whether in marriage or friendship, is conversation.*
>
> OSCAR WILDE

A FAMOUS QUOTE once said that "women are from Venus and men are from Mars". The differences between men and women are so diverse, that they might as well be residents from different planets. From their genetic makeups to the way they handle day-to-day situations, males and females have marked differences from each other.

Understanding these differences is one of the keys to ensuring a marriage survives. While there are some slight differences from one person to the next, this chapter will talk about the general differences between men and women. Understanding these differences and knowing how to handle them can spell the difference between a happy marriage and an unhappy one.

Communication differences between men and women

Since this book mainly focuses on communication, it is simply appropriate that we first talk about the communication differences of men and women. Regardless of what your sex is, it is almost a guarantee that you got into a fight with your spouse even if you never really meant to do anything wrong.

While a lot of these fights are caused by misunderstandings and the failure to say what you mean, some of these fights can actually be caused by non-recognition of the various communication differences between men and women. Here is a simplified list of some of the differences between the sexes in terms of basic communication.

1. Reasons for talking

The reason men communicate is rooted in a specific purpose. The moves of men in general are oriented towards something specific, and this is evident in their conversation style. When they talk, they are always aiming to achieve something or they want to make a point. They use communication as a means to achieve that means, and they want to achieve it as soon as possible. It's partly why men tend to be more direct to the point.

The reason women communicate is mainly to make sense of what they want to say. While men talk because they already have something in mind, women tend to use communication as a means to help themselves make sense of what they are thinking and feeling. More than just a means to communicate something, women also see conversations as their opportunity to release negative feelings and strengthen their bond with their spouse or whoever they are talking to.

2. How much needs to be said

Men in general are oriented towards productivity and efficiency, and this can manifest with the way they handle conversations. When they start talking, often times they have already organized what they have to say, and so they do it in a quick and organized manner.

They often share the things they think is important, and will often cut the conversation if they think they already know the point of conversation or what needs to be done. Given that women do not always talk this way, this can be a potential source of annoyance for the men.

Reiterating what was said on the previous item, women tend to use conversation as a means to gather their thoughts and arrive to what they want to say. Beyond being able to communicate what they want to say, what women are looking for is someone to listen. This is why they highly appreciate it if men would listen and understand what they feel.

3. Way of Listening

Men have a different approach to listening compared to women. Men are more attuned to listen actively. Often times, when they talk to someone, they presume that something needs to be done, and they listen to conversations in an effort to uncover what that something is. Men listen with the intent to do something, often in the form of advice or assistance. Because they are wired like this, some men find it a little difficult to stay patient while listening to their partner.

Women, on the other hand, do not listen with a specific solution as an end result. For them, the fact that they are there to listen to begin with is already something. For them, being there to hear out their partner's concerns is their way to show that they care.

It is also the reason why they consider it so important that their partner should listen to their concerns, no matter how mundane it might seem. If a solution is arrived to after the conversation, that is considered already as a bonus.

4. Approach to his/her own problems

When men are facing problems, they have the tendency to keep it to themselves. As much as possible, they look to deal with it alone, either by finding a solution or just going for a temporary escape. This is one of the reasons why when some men deal with problems, they commonly retreat to a place where they are comfortable.

They can go on a vacation, lock themselves up in their room, or tend to their hobbies. It's their means to calm themselves down in a stressful situation while they make sense of the problem.

While men value their me-time when they feel embattled, women have the tendency to seek outside help. Using words as their means to make sense of what they are feeling, they value conversations when they are facing problems of any kind.

Instead of being withdrawn, they actively seek

advice and comfort from people they know they can trust. When they see that the person they are talking to about their problems is listening to them, they highly value that, even if they don't come up with a solution right away.

5. Approach to his/her spouse's problems

When the wife says she has a problem or if he notices it himself, the man swoops down to action right away. He wants to help his wife right away and wants to find the solution to the problem as soon as possible.

Beyond their nature as a person that seeks for solutions, men would love nothing else than to provide help and companionship for their spouse. This approach can sometimes backfire though, as women may sometimes feel they are too aggressive and/or do not put their emotions into consideration.

When the husband has a problem, the wife has the tendency to push for a conversation. This is because as mentioned earlier, the wife expects their husband to be there when they have problems, so they do the same for them.

There is always the chance for the man to be more withdrawn, as they tend to avoid outside help when they are dealing with problems. This can have a negative effect on the woman, as they may feel that she is "losing" her husband.

6. What frustrates them during conversations

There are many things that can frustrate men during conversations. The biggest source of frustration for them is when they feel that they are being told what to do. He doesn't appreciate it when his competence is being questioned or if his problem is being dismissed as too small.

When this happens, they have the tendency to withdraw even further, canceling the conversation altogether or express their displeasure in other ways. As such, the best way to approach a man when conversing is to resist the temptation of telling him what to do.

At the same time, there are many things that can frustrate women during conversations. Perhaps the biggest peeve they have is when they feel that the person they are talking to do not put importance to what they are saying.

They don't like being ignored and they don't like their ideas or concerns being dismissed as unimportant. As such, men should avoid talking to women with a dismissive tone. They get turned off by the conversation once men start to say that their problems are not significant or if they are told that they are being too emotional.

The Takeaway

- Men and women have multiple differences, and it is reflected with the way they communicate.
- Men and women have different ways of approaching their problems. While men usually keep it within themselves, women often seek for ways to vocalize their problems.
- Men and women also have different approaches when they hear their spouse is having problems. Men often go and look for solutions, while women prioritize hearing out the sentiments of the person they are talking to.
- Men and women also get frustrated by specific things during conversations. Men don't like being told what to do, and women don't like not being taken seriously.

There are all kinds of problems that can saddle a marriage. However, some factors prove to be more common sources of problems than others. In the next chapter, we will talk about some of the most common sources of problems for couples and some of the best solutions for each.

THREE
COMMON PROBLEMS AND THE BEST WAYS TO HANDLE THEM

> *It is sometimes essential for a husband and wife to quarrel – they get to know each other better.*
>
> GOETHE

MARRIED COUPLES CAN FACE a lot of problems over the course of their partnership. Some of them can be already present even before they got married, while others are only exclusively present when living the married life. While each couple face a unique set of problems, some factors cause more problems for most couples than others.

For the benefit of couples everywhere, this chapter will talk about some of the most common problems married couples face. At the same time, this chapter will also show solutions on how couples can approach and resolve them. Never let these common problem sources drive a wedge between you and your partner.

Family

Considering that marriages are essentially the fusion of two different family lines, it is inevitable that the families of the couple will play a big role in the success of their marriage.

Each individual is raised differently by their families, and that contributes on their view on how their marriage should work moving forward.

Issues can arise when family members start to meddle with the couple's affairs. At the same time, specific families operate under specific norms and values. These differences can present problems for a married couple, intentional or otherwise, and may prevent a marriage from reaching its full potential.

Even though your family and your partner's family may be worlds different from one another, there are still ways for the marriage to work. You don't have to detach your marriage from your respective families because doing so would only cause more harm than good.

Respecting family members of the spouse, together with their norms and beliefs, is one way to make the marriage work. Also, making a conscious effort to get along with the spouse's family will be beneficial. Listen to what they have to say on different matters, but not to the point that they are already dictating what you should do as a couple.

Your (and your partner's) extended family can be a source of conflict for you as a married couple. However, it's also possible for them to become one of your best allies. The best way to manage this is to give the families the respect they deserve, while retaining your independence as a couple.

Religion

Religion has always been one of the stickiest issues to talk about with other people. Together with other contentious topics such as politics, religion has its way of creating a division between two people. It is not uncommon for couples to have different religious beliefs, even before they get married.

While some people are able to find a common ground in spite of their religious differences, others don't. For some married couples, religious differences even end up as a major source of conflict and become grounds for an eventual separation.

Managing religious differences between married

couples is never easy, but it has been done countless of times before.

Following a certain form of faith is a very personal decision, and in many ways puts a strain on the relationships involved.

The easiest way to resolve this would be for the couple to adapt the same religion. However, no one should be forced to follow a certain religion, lest more discontent will come out of it. Interfaith marriages are possible, but they are considered the exception rather than the rule.

Regardless of whether the couple decides to follow their spouse's faith or not, mutual respect and tolerance between the two parties should be present.

Loss of sex drive

This may not seem like a big deal for some married couples, but there are marriages that were dissolved because of incompatibilities when it comes to sex. The loss of sex drive is a natural phenomenon that can be caused by multiple factors. As people grow older, both men and women have reduced production of hormones, which drastically affects their sex drive.

Also, the commitments of either party (such as work and children) can take away a lot of time and energy, making them "too busy and tired" for sex.

Lastly, people who are having extramarital affairs tend to lose their sex drive towards their spouses, as their drive is directed towards another person.

The loss of sex drive can cause all kinds of problems for married couples. Fortunately, there are many ways to resolve the potential problems that dwindling sex drive can cause.

First, you need to talk about what causes your sexual problems, if there are any. Sometimes, the problem can be solved by spending time with each other, or by understanding that our bodies change as we age.

Also, maintaining fidelity is critical, as extramarital affairs are seen to contribute to loss of libido towards your partner.

Perhaps the most important thing is to recognize that married life goes beyond just sex. You can always love each other even when you make love less often.

Finances

Some would argue that money is the main reason why couples are having conflicts. Any married couple can attest that managing day-to-day expenses is one of the "dirty jobs" of married life. Of course, food must be available on the table, household expenses need to be paid, and children should receive their needs such as education.

There are other things to consider such as health care, insurance, properties, and the like. Given this, the ability of the couple to provide for the needs of the family and how they do it have a great impact on the marriage itself.

There are a number of common problems married couples encounter when it comes to finances. There are times when the combined income of the couple is not enough to sustain the family's needs and expenses. Also, the way both parties spend the money can cause conflicts. Another potential problem source is with regards to how much of each side's income goes to the household.

While such problems can be overwhelming, solutions are also readily available. It is best for both sides to be transparent in the way they earn and handle money.

Developing good spending practices is also crucial, especially now that the financial demands for married couple is starkly different from single individuals.

Unmet Expectations

When people get married, they have expectations for themselves, their partners, and their marriage.

While some expectations are accomplished or even exceeded, others are actually not met for one reason or another. Unmet expectations put a lot of strain on married couples, whether these expectations are realistic or not. These expectations can cause fights and lead to a feeling of discontent.

The best way to avoid unmet expectations is to set realistic ones. A lot of couples create expectations as a couple and as individuals that are simply unrealistic. Doing so will only lead to disappointment. When creating your list of expectations, ask yourself: "are these expectations realistic and achievable?"

Perhaps just as important as creating realistic expectations is to simply develop contentment. It is important for couples to learn to appreciate what they have in their partner and their marriage, and not focus on what is not there. Lastly, there is always a nicer way to say that your partner needs to improve on something.

Affairs

Since the beginning of time, immorality has always been among the biggest obstacles to healthy marriages. There are many reasons why people get involved in affairs. Some people see it as a means to boost their self-esteem; others do it because they see qualities in other people that they don't see in their partner. There are also people who cheat because they already had enough of their partner.

An affair has incredibly disastrous effects: it can break up families, destroy marriages beyond repair, and even lead to lengthy legal disputes. In spite of all this, affairs are still relatively common, and both men and women get involved in such scenarios.

So how should married couples deal with affairs? Given the destructive consequences of having an affair, the best way to deal with it is thru avoidance. No matter how good or bad your relationship is going, settling for an extramarital relationship is never the answer.

Fidelity is one of the keys to a successful marriage. Compromising your marriage for something that might be temporary at best is never a good idea. However, what if adultery was already committed? Fortunately for couples, there are still solutions. It always starts with forgiveness from both parties. From there, the one who committed adultery should find ways to fix the marriage, and the other party should give him/her a fair chance to do it.

Jealousy and Insecurity

Considered to be twin emotions, a combination of jealousy and insecurity can undermine even the strongest of relationships. These two emotions can be rooted in various factors, which may or may not be the fault of the spouse.

It is easy to be jealous and insecure if the spouse cheats and/or make their partner feel inferior. There are also situations wherein it's not the spouse's fault why they feel jealous or insecure. It can be caused by personal inadequacies or previous negative experiences. Regardless of the cause, excessive jealousy and insecurity can ruin a marriage.

So how should you deal with jealousy and insecurity? It all starts with identifying the root of such emotions. Ask your spouse why he or she is feeling jealous or insecure, telling him or her in the least hostile way possible. From there, listen carefully to his or her answer. Once you know the root of the jealousy, it will be up to you to make the necessary changes.

For example, if his or her jealousy is caused by you flirting with other people, stop these illicit affairs right away. If his or her feelings of insecurity are caused by how you treat him, make the necessary adjustments to your behavior. The solutions to jealousy and insecurity can vary, but any married couple can overcome it as long as they stay together throughout.

Children

Children are considered to be the crown jewels of married couples. However, the presence (or even the absence) of children can be a source of conflict for married couples.

It takes time and money to raise kids well. The growing pains of the children can put a strain on the parents.

Couples can disagree on matters on how to raise their children, from the methods of disciplining them to the kinds of activities they can participate in. Some couples are even getting in an unspoken competition against each other of "who's the better parent". Raising children is a difficult task, it is arguably more difficult now more than ever before, and that is putting a lot of strain in marriages everywhere.

Being a parent is never going to be easy. However, I believe that this task should not be harder than it already is, and it certainly should never serve as the wedge that tears marriages apart.

The first thing the couple should understand is that parenting should be a team effort. It is never a competition to see who the better parent is, or a matter of whose parenting principle is better.

Your ultimate goal as parents is that your children grow up to be the best adult they can possibly be, and the best way to achieve that is by working together. If you have disagreements on how to raise your kids, it's best to talk it out. Lastly, the rigors of parenting should never mean that you'll have no time for each other.

Jobs

This can be a sticky situation, considering that work is vital in keeping any marriage afloat. It helps in keeping the household financially stable, and it gives the person a sense of progress and personal development. However, there is always such a thing that "too much of a good thing is bad". A person's work and business interests can put a strain on a marriage in so many ways.

Work can occupy so much time that people start to have less time for their marriage and family. Also, their line of work (ex: what their job is or where they work) can create conflict. Lastly, the revenue they get from such jobs and businesses, whether it is sufficient or not, can cause couples to fight.

Fortunately, there are many solutions available if

your work is becoming a source of your marital problems. The best way to manage this issue is to establish a proper work-life balance. You need to tend to your job or business, but you need to make sure that it doesn't come at the cost of family time. Improving work efficiency gives you more time to spend with your spouse and family.

Setting aside time for them will also work wonders. Even a simple letter or phone call when you're away from home will help keep your bond with your family strong. In short, balancing priorities and making time for your marriage and family are essential for the marriage to work.

Stagnancy

Even the best marriages can hit a snag along the way. Stagnancy is one of the biggest enemies of a marriage. A marriage becomes stagnant when they stop growing as a couple. When a marriage becomes stagnant, the couple stops creating new memories, enjoying experiences, and sharing love. They get bored of each other, and the things that used to excite them don't excite them as much anymore.

When a marriage becomes too stagnant, there may come a time when either side (or even both sides) of the marriage will drift apart. You cannot underestimate stagnancy; a lot of couples look elsewhere because they've become "bored" of their marriage!

There are many ways to combat stagnancy in a marriage. One of the ways to do it is to try something new every now and then. This is because when things become too repetitive, there is a tendency for the couple to get bored. Trying new things together adds to the married life experience, and is also a great way to break the monotony of daily married life.

Another way is to always find ways to show affection to your spouse. You can never be too old for some TLC (Tender Loving Care). Giving and receiving affection is one of the best ways to keep the passion alive as the marriage advances in age.

The Takeaway

- Married couples face a long list of potential problems. From how to raise their family to personal insecurities, a lot of things can put a strain in relationships.
- Both you and your partner shouldn't underestimate nor overestimate your problems. It is important to take action when warranted.
- There are many ways to take on these

common problems. However, it is important that regardless of the problem, you should be in it together.

THERE ARE all kinds of problems that can put marriages to the test. But do you really understand the problems you are having? It is important that you have a full understanding of your problems as a couple. From there, you can create solutions that will hopefully resolve them.

In the next chapter, we will talk about understanding your problems as a couple and approaches that will help in resolving them.

FOUR
UNDERSTANDING AND CHANGING WHAT'S WRONG

> *When you stop expecting people to be perfect, you can like them for who they are.*
>
> DONALD MILLER

RECOGNIZING what is wrong in your relationship is just the first step in resolving them. A lot of married couples end up in divorce because they weren't able to handle it well.

What's even worse, some couples end up separating because they saw problems in their relationship and chose to do nothing about them.

When you identify things that are going wrong in your marriage, both parties should make the necessary steps to understand and resolve them.

Understanding and changing what's wrong is

important to keep marriages healthy. There are many ways to approach marital problems and to keep the relationship alive. This chapter will discuss some of the ways to do it.

1. Handling anger and conflicts

The most successful couples do not necessarily have to never fight. In fact, they do fight just like all of us! They are human after all, prone to get angry from time to time. However, what sets healthy marriages apart from unhealthy ones is how they are able to handle their conflicts and keep their anger from destroying their relationship. Here are some ways on how couples can properly handle anger and conflicts so that their marriage will stay healthy.

One of the most important things married couples should understand is that even while in the middle of a major conflict, they should remain connected and engaged with each other. There would be times when couples just agree to disagree, and there are times when emotions would just bubble over the surface.

However, in the middle of a conflict, the best way to handle things is to do it with love. Refrain from saying stuff that you know will be hurtful to your spouse. Never forget to show affection to your spouse during and after a quarrel, and never forget to respect your partner no matter what.

Also, when you are in the middle of an argument, you should focus on the issue at hand. Some couples tend to attack the person, which is a destructive habit in both short and long terms. Both of you should refrain from doing that. Instead, you should focus on what your argument is all about.

Is that even worth arguing about? Are there solutions available for you to explore? Can either or both sides do better the next time around? Focus on finding solutions to your arguments. That way, your fight can even end up strengthening your bond as a couple.

Never forget to apologize after an argument, especially if you have said some unsatisfactory things to your spouse or when things got a little too heated up. I have witnessed more than a few marriages and relationships that were doomed because of one side not saying sorry to the other.

A more detailed discussion on forgiving and letting go is found later in this chapter, but this process can begin with a simple "I'm sorry". If you find this difficult, remind yourself that your marriage is still more important than your pride.

2. Solving problems

As mentioned earlier, any marriage will face their fair share of problems. More than just handling conflicts, strong couples know how to manage problems, however big or small it may be.

So what makes a couple great problem solvers? There is no exact formula for it, but there are specific traits that couples with strong problem management skills have. These include, but not limited to: knowledge of their partner and the ability to stay connected even when pressures are mounting.

An intimate knowledge of your partner greatly helps in managing conflicts. Sometimes, it is not enough that you know how to take on problems. You also have to know how your partner takes on these problems. A deep knowledge of your partner's personality and problem management style helps you push the right buttons at the right time.

When you know these details, you know how to best approach your partner, how to talk to them, and how you can make them listen. Knowledge of your partner is not enough to solve all of your marital problems, but it puts you in a better position to solve them.

Knowing and developing a conflict management style is also a great way to resolve most of your marital issues. Of course, developing this style takes time, and yours may be different from other couples. It starts with understanding how you and your partner manage conflicts, as well as being familiar with each other's behavioral tendencies.

From there, you will figure out which strategies work and which don't. With experience and familiarity with each other, you can formulate a way to manage just about every kind of conflict without unnecessarily hurting each other.

Perhaps the most important thing couples must learn is that you should stay connected with each other, even when you are facing mounting problems. There are some conflicts wherein you literally cannot stand each other.

In spite of these problems, there are three rules that you should follow when you are in a fight.

1. Never be too resentful that you keep holding grudges long after the fight is done with.
2. Never be too passive that you try and avoid every issue that needs to be resolved.
3. Never stop caring for your spouse.

3. Recreating Intimacy

Intimacy is a very important element in any marriage. In fact, it is one of the things that make a marriage stand out over basically every kind of relationship out there! A couple that is intimate with one another has a unique bond that cannot be compared with anything else out there.

In contrast, a marriage that has lost its intimacy is basically a dying one. You need to keep that intimacy burning like it's the first time you've met each other. If you or your partner feel that you are losing it, it is important that you make the effort to regain it. This is where recreating intimacy comes into the picture.

The first, and perhaps the most important step, in recreating intimacy that was lost for whatever reason is for the couple to make time for each other. This makes a lot of sense in many ways. After all, how can you be intimate with someone when you barely have the time to be together and build any sort of togetherness?

Both marriage experts and counselors agree that lack of time is one of the reasons why intimacy fades. As such, I recommend that if you want to rebuild the intimacy that you have as a couple, spend more time together. Talk to each other, even while over meals. Set aside some time where you can be together. It all boils down to making time for your partner.

Beyond making time for each other, it is important that you make good use of whatever time you have together. There is a reason why spending time together is called "quality time". The question is, are you spending your time together with quality? A lot of people think that setting aside a "special day" for their partner, such as going on a vacation or a lavish date, already counts as "quality time".

It actually goes beyond that. Your time together should contain meaningful interaction, especially if you don't really spend too much time together. Talk to your spouse. Ask them how their day is. Listen to their stories. Hear out their problems. Express your love. That is quality time.

Another way to recreate intimacy is to resolve whatever conflicts you have with each other. One of the most common reasons why couples become distant to each other is conflict. Unresolved conflicts have a way of developing a wedge between couples.

Think of it this way; if you have a problem with someone, you don't like something about him/her, or you simply hate them, you would rather avoid them than to stay close with them, right? As such, one of the first steps in reviving intimacy between couples is to fix whatever conflicts you have with each other. Resolving conflict will go a long way in reviving a couple's desire to spend more time together.

It is important that you help your spouse heal his or her own wounds. Let's face it, our partner is never going to be perfect. Expecting him or her to be perfect will only set you up for disappointment, and will put unreasonable pressure and expectations on your partner.

The person may have character flaws and insecurities that you may not know before you got married. As a spouse, it's not your responsibility to tolerate or fight these inadequacies. Rather, it's your responsibility to accept and understand these limitations, and help your partner in resolving them if possible.

4. Repairing broken trust

Trust is one of the most important elements in a marriage, or in any form of relationship for that matter. When trust is broken for whatever reason, or if the person refuses to give trust to another, the relationship disintegrates. Inaction to this matter can hasten the downfall of your marriage. It is important that married couples keep their trust to each other.

So how can you repair broken trust? It is not going to be easy, but it is 100% doable.

To begin the healing of broken trust, it is important for both sides to forgive. The problem is that a number of couples refuse to forgive each other for a myriad of reasons, and it's basically the reason why their trust for each other refuses to heal.

Forgiving will be discussed in detail in a later part of this book, but it is important to know that rebuilding broken trust starts with forgiveness from both sides. It doesn't matter who's wrong or right, who caused the hurt first, or whatever. To begin the healing, one must learn how to forgive first.

The next step to repairing broken trust is for the couple to be honest with each other. A lot of people would say that they don't trust their spouse, and they won't even bother to tell them why. Because of this, the couple resolves nothing, trust remains broken, and they keep on hating their spouse for reasons they may not even understand.

It is important that you discuss with each other why you think they are not worthy of your trust. Both of you deserve nothing less than honest answers, so make sure to respond to each other truthfully.

The next step to repairing broken trust is to give each other a chance. A lot of marriages go down the drain because while they say that they have forgiven their spouse for the things they did wrong, they have never let go of what had happened. The pain lives within them, and it puts the other person in eternal condemnation.

When you forgive, give the other person a chance

to prove they have changed and to show their worth. At the same time, your spouse should also learn to forgive you and give you the opportunity to show that you mean it. Forgiveness takes time, character, and love. However, this is attainable if both sides are willing to do whatever it takes.

If you are asking for forgiveness, you need to mean it. One of the more famous quotes would tell you that "Say what you do and do what you say". The problem with most people is when they ask for forgiveness, they would sooner or later do it again. When you ask for the forgiveness of your spouse, you need to make sure that the mistake never happens again.

5. Creating shared meaning

Having shared meaning is an important component in strong marriages. However, what does shared meaning actually mean? According to John and Julie Gottman, shared meaning is **something that the couple creates together and is something that is unique to every couple**.

This can be explained by the corollary of the house and a home. A home is a house, but a house doesn't necessarily equate to a home. Any house can be transformed into a home, as long as there is love and security within it. When a couple has shared meaning, even things that seem ordinary on the surface mean something to the couple, and that galvanizes the couple even more.

The first step in creating a shared meaning together is to create a shared vision together. Actually, the roots of this vision are already there even before you get married, even as early as when you are still getting to know each other. This vision consists of your ideals as a couple, the things that you prioritize, and the plans that you have for each other and your family in the long run.

When creating this vision, there are important things to remember: look at the big picture, keep things realistic, and it should further strengthen your relationship.

There is no exact science when it comes to creating shared meaning. Many couples create it even when they don't plan to, and there are also couples who can't create it even when they consciously make the effort to make one. One of the most important ingredients of creating this shared meaning is time.

When you spend time with each other, you are able to create lasting memories and you gain a better perspective on what you want with your marriage moving forward. Building a shared meaning is always a work in progress, but it takes a couple that is committed to each other to create one that will define your marriage.

Building a shared meaning also involves an ever-involving understanding of the individuals involved. It is a fact that individuals are raised differently, have different sets of ideas and priorities, and have different experiences that formed their identities.

There are times when these differences would create compatibility issues. The good news is that most of these differences can be resolved, as long as the couple remains on the same page. A positive mindset, a strong friendship, and mutual respect are essential to overcome conflicts and strengthen a marriage's identity.

6. Keeping love alive for the long-term

Looking at one side, love is responsible for keeping couples together. On another perspective, people would say that love is not enough to sustain a marriage. While both perspectives are true in their own ways, basically everyone would agree that love is an important component in any successful marriage.

A couple that has no love for each other has no other recourse than to go on separate ways. A lot of couples have been asking how they can keep love alive for the long term. Perhaps, it's recognition of the importance of love in any marriage. Here are some ways to keep love alive.

The first step to keeping love alive is to show constant appreciation. One of the things most couples forget as their marriage grows older is that they forget to show appreciation for their spouse. Your spouse will eventually start to wonder if he or she is still important to you, and that can accelerate the decline in your marriage.

It will break anyone's heart if they feel that they are not appreciated by the person they love. Before it even gets to that point, make it a habit to appreciate your partner. Always thank them for the things they do for you. Always tell and show that you love them. Surprise them every once in a while.

Also, you got to fight apathy. It was once said that apathy, more than hate, is the biggest enemy of love. Apathy can arise from a wide variety of things. It can arise from various elements such as unresolved conflicts, stress, and negative attitudes from you and/or your partner. You stop caring for the marriage, you start drifting elsewhere, and eventually you lose your love for your partner.

So what is the best antidote for apathy? Add more variety to your everyday activities. Don't be afraid to get out of your routine. Have fun together. Show your love in both big and small ways. All these things can help you keep apathy out of the way.

Keep an attitude of gratitude in your marriage. When you feel like your marriage is going south, think of it this way: not everyone gets to have a happy marriage and not everyone gets to be in love with a person as awesome as your spouse.

Don't allow yourself to be desensitized to the great things they do for you. Never forget your spouse, even if there are all kinds of wonderful things happening in your everyday life. Being grateful is one of the best ways to keep your marriage afloat.

7. How to forgive and let go

Forgiveness is important in a marriage. The fact is, your spouse is going to make mistakes every once in a while. They would even hurt you and leave your heart broken. A lot of people know that forgiving someone you love is crucial, but not everyone is willing or able to do it.

In fact, there are some people who find it even more difficult to forgive the people they love. One of the hallmarks of strong marriages is their ability to forgive each other and keep moving forward. Learn how to forgive and let go; your marriage will be better off with it.

Not everyone would be willing to admit that they haven't forgiven a person. Even married couples tend to never admit to their spouses that they are unhappy with them until they decide to leave them behind.

How can you know if you have ill feelings about your spouse? There is legitimate resent towards your spouse, and you express this resentment when you are with them or with others.

You also keep bringing up their flaws, their mistakes, and the hurts they have caused you in the past. It eventually comes to the point that you literally can't stand their presence and the emotion you feel when you see them (or even hear a mention of them) is anger.

After the admission comes the process of forgiveness and letting go. First, try to understand why you are feeling the grudge that you feel. After making sense of the feeling, consider if you played a role you played in that hurtful event. Take responsibility for whatever mistakes you may have done and stay away from the vicious cycle of hate that consumes you even with the mere sight of your spouse.

Forgive the person, even if they may have zero plans of apologizing to you. Let go of the overwhelming desire to accomplish revenge. Finally, live in the present and enjoy whatever is still in front of you, which includes your spouse and your married life together.

Beyond healing, it also pays to be proactive and just avoid picking up grudges altogether. It pays to be more understanding of your spouse. He may not have the desire to hurt or disappoint you, and there are reasons why such undesirable outcomes happened.

It pays to have more empathy, to look at things in the eyes of the other person. Perhaps most importantly, you got to learn to be forgiving and compassionate in your everyday life. Learn to forgive other people right away, and learn to forgive yourself too while you're at it. Life becomes much better if there are no grudges that bear you down.

The Takeaway

- All kinds of things can go wrong in your marriage. The first step in resolving these problems is to actually recognize that they exist.
- There will always be conflicts in married life. You should learn to handle them the right way. Staying connected with each other, avoiding the temptation to attack

each other, and saying sorry are some of the best ways to defuse marital problems.
- Great problem solving skills is one of the hallmarks of a successful marriage. An intimate knowledge of your partner and developing conflict management skills are ways to quash conflicts before they cause damage.
- Intimacy is an important element in marriage that is often lost when the couple is at odds with each other. Revive it by making time for each other, expressing your love regularly, and resolving problems that pull you apart from each other.
- Fixing broken trust is important in keeping marriages alive. Forgiveness, giving each other a chance, and following through with your promises are some of the ways to revive trust.
- Shared meaning is one of the things that make marriages strong. There is no exact science in building this, but creating a shared vision, understanding the values of each individual, and creating good memories together.
- Forgiveness is very important for resolving all kinds of conflict. Let go of previous

hurts and give your spouse a chance to prove himself/herself. Also, you should avoid having grudges altogether.

In the next chapter, we are going to take your communication skills to the next level. There is strong value to communication in marriage, but are you using it the right way? You're about to learn how to do communication right.

FIVE
COMMUNICATION SKILLS MASTERY

> *The art of conversation lies in listening.*
>
> MALCOLM FORBES

EFFECTIVE COMMUNICATION IS essential in our everyday lives. It can help you get virtually everywhere you need to go, and it can help you to accomplish everything you need to accomplish. Not many people may think of it this way, but developing good communication skills also bodes well for a marriage.

We have been hammering over and over again that better communication can save an ailing marriage and can strengthen an already-thriving one. The importance of communication in marriage has been mostly discussed in the early parts of this book.

Now, this chapter focuses on how you can build

your communication skills. These pointers will help you develop different aspects of your communication technique to improve your interaction with your spouse. To further simplify things, I decided to compile this list in a dos and don'ts format, so you know exactly what to do every time you talk to your partner.

Learn the Dos of communicating with your spouse

1. Learn active listening

Active listening is a vital skill, especially when it comes to married couples. Learning how to listen actively will greatly improve your talks, make your partner feel more appreciated, and defuse feuds before they even explode.

So how can you do active listening right? First, you should not just wait for your turn to speak. Instead, concentrate on what your partner has to say and try to understand it. To help you out, you can use techniques such as repeating what they said or asking questions for clarification. Lastly, resist the urge to comment or counter what they said, at least not until they are done in airing their side.

2. Pay attention to nonverbal cues

Paying attention to nonverbal cues is one of the most overlooked communication tricks in the book. A lot can be said by the person that they may not be able to express in words. You can tell their emotions and feelings by their facial expressions, their body language, and their level of urgency when they talk.

Pay attention to their nonverbal cues and you'll get a hint on what to expect and how you should proceed with the conversation. At the same time, you should pay attention to your own nonverbal cues. For example, some nonverbal cues such as looking away and focusing on something else show disinterest, which can derail your conversation very quickly.

3. Establish eye contact

According to many experts, eye contact is the most important element of nonverbal communication. A lot of meaning can be derived from the way a person looks (or doesn't look) at another. Just take a look at these examples.

An inability to look in the eye of the other person can be interpreted as a sign of being uneasy. A sharp look can be a sign of anger, defiance, or a strong eagerness to get a point across. When talking to your spouse, you got to take note of the emotion in your eyes. As for you, practice making eye contact with your partner when you talk as it's interpreted as a sign of integrity, sincerity, and a willingness to continue with the conversation.

4. Encourage

You cannot underestimate the power of encouragement when you talk. Creating a mood and environment that encourages speaking out inspires confidence, gets meaningful conversations moving, and prevents couples from becoming emotionally distant. Improving your communication in marriage can be as simple as encouraging your partner to speak out their thoughts, whether it concerns your marriage or not.

If your partner is feeling awkward or they can't find the words, encourage them by showing you are willing to listen. Offer positive words when they are feeling bad. Make them feel that it's OK for him/her to talk to you anytime, no matter what the topic is.

5. Diplomacy and fairness is important

It pays to be diplomatic when you are talking to your spouse. There would always be disagreements, whether big or small, when you are together in a single household. Instead of taking an approach wherein you got to win every single argument, the better approach is to take each other's feedback into consideration.

Also, give each other a fair chance to speak their mind. No matter how outrageous their statement may be or how opposite it is from your personal preference, hear out your partner. Create a conversational environment that encourages diplomacy and fairness. Your conversations as a couple will be better off with it. Of course, it all starts with you.

6. Express feelings and needs

A healthy marriage is where both husband and wife can freely express their feelings and needs. It is important that you never hold back on what you have to say. Honesty is a virtue that is valued in all levels of relationships, and this is especially true in marriage. It is important that you create a culture wherein the concerns of both sides are freely expressed.

Practice speaking out to your partner if you are the silent type. If your partner is the silent type, encourage them to talk. Both sides should have the green light to air their concerns, and both should listen to what the other has to say.

7. Consider the other person's perspective

Different people have different perspectives. Learning empathy, the ability to look at scenarios and conversations from the perspective of the other person, is vital to understanding these perspectives. Building empathy will help you better understand both the verbal and nonverbal elements of what your partner says.

Also, being empathic is a great way to show that you care about the person and what they are saying. So how can you show empathy to your spouse? First, put an emphasis on listening. Second, analyze what they just said instead of reacting right away. Lastly, make it a habit to care more for others.

8. Manage your tone and watch your words

The words you say and the manner in which you deliver them greatly affects how your message will end up being interpreted. In that regard, there are two basic things you need to remember when talking to your spouse or anyone for that matter: manage your tone and watch your words.

As much as possible, avoid shouting at people and don't use words that are hurtful and/or insulting to the person. I know this is exceptionally difficult to do, especially when tensions are high. It takes a lot of grace and self-control to be able to check both of these in the heat of the moment. However, you can master this with the help of practice and discipline.

9. Set distractions aside

When talking to your spouse, there are all kinds of things that can prove to be distractions. From prior commitments to that mobile device, these distractions can get in the way of great conversations. In some cases, it can be outright disrespectful to your spouse!

I know a lot of fights breaking out between couples because their spouse is paying attention to their phone while they are saying something! It is important that you keep distractions to a minimum when you talk or discuss something important.

10. Be prepared

Being ready is one of the best ways to improve your conversations. It would be nice if you can prepare before you talk to your spouse, especially if you are about to talk about something very important.

First, you have to settle your thoughts, thinking of what you need to say before you say it.

Second, anticipate any potential questions or reactions your spouse may have with the conversation.

Third, keep your emotions in check, especially if it's making you feel angry.

Lastly, think of how you would open and close your talk. While there's no way to perfectly prepare for a conversation as they are dynamic by nature, being prepared will help you get your message across properly.

Learn the don'ts of communicating with your spouse

1. Don't dig up the past

One of the most common things I've observed with quarreling couples is the constant bringing up of the past. They look up the previous mistakes of their partner and then throw it in their faces. Not only is this approach super annoying, but it also shows a gross act of immaturity.

It also shows that you may not have totally forgiven your partner for their past mistakes, which is never a good sign for both now and the future of your marriage. When talking to your spouse, refrain from the habit of digging up the past. Nothing good has ever come out of it.

2. Don't attack your spouse

This is a very common incidence in couples that are quarreling. Attacking your spouse not only worsens the argument, but also pulls down the level of discourse between the two of you. This habit does not resolve anything, and can wear down even the strongest of couples.

While criticizing your partner from time to time is good, criticizing them too much, especially if your aim is to prove that you're right and he/she is not, does not bring anything good. When in the middle of an argument, resist the temptation to attack your spouse. When arguing, both of you must focus on the problem, not on the person.

3. Don't assume they can read your mind

One of the common pitfalls of couples everywhere is that they expect their partners to know everything. One of the most common reasons why couples fight is because the other person assumed that their partner already knows what they are trying to say.

Even if you've been together for a long time, you can't expect your partners to be mind readers. So what is the better approach here? When you talk, it pays to be specific. When you argue, speak your mind. Don't presume that your partner knows everything, because more often than not, they don't.

4. Don't resort to avoidance

Some couples resort to avoidance when they are approaching a point of conflict. There are many reasons for this phenomenon. It can be because the person is simply passive by nature. It can also be because the person has become tired of countless unresolved arguments. It can also be because the person feels like their partner is never listening to them.

Whatever the root cause, resorting to avoidance can only lead to more trouble moving forward. Problems are left unresolved, conflicts stay simmering, and feelings become repressed. For the both of you, while I don't encourage being overly aggressive in conversations, you should never resort to avoidance.

5. Don't be destructive

Criticism can be extremely destructive if done the wrong way and if done for the wrong reasons. Criticism is never healthy if it is reeking with sarcasm, insults, or anything that is below the belt. Also, it is never good if the conversation ends up into an exercise of blaming and faultfinding.

When criticizing, you should aim to build up the person, not break them down further. Also, excessive criticism of the person is never good. It can get extremely burdensome for them. Lastly, never criticize your partner just to win an argument or prove that you're better.

6. Don't let toxic conversations linger

In every couple, there are conversations that end up becoming toxic for one reason or another. Regardless of the reasons, you should never let them linger. Toxic conversations that are unresolved hang over a couple like a dark cloud, taking away joy from them while leaving open gaps that can serve as roots for bigger problems.

When faced with a toxic conversation, ask yourself this: Is the conversation even worth proceeding with? If it's not even worth talking about, then end the issue right away. If the conversation is relevant, actively participate and collaborate with your partner to arrive at the best outcomes.

The Takeaway

- Effective communication can serve as one

of the core elements of a successful marriage. Both you and your partner must be involved for it to work.
- There are some things that you must do when you are communicating with your spouse. These include using active listening, paying attention to what they say and do, having empathy, and being prepared.
- There are also some things that you should not do when you are communicating with your spouse. Resorting to personal attacks, being avoidant, and assuming they can read your mind are not helpful.

Now that you have mastered the art of communication, the next step is to give your marriage a complete overhaul. There are various steps that you can use to take your marriage to the next level. The next chapter focuses on proven steps that will improve your marriage in all aspects.

SIX
PROVEN ACTIONS TO IMPROVE YOUR RELATIONSHIP

> *A marriage requires falling in love many times, always with the same person.*
>
> MIGNON MCLAUGHLIN

IT DOESN'T MATTER if you are a newlywed or you have been together for 50 years. It doesn't matter if you are a high-profile couple or a low-key one. Regardless of the type of marriage you have or the current state of it, there is always room for improvement.

Toxic marriages that are on the verge of breaking down can always start over and make things better for themselves. Meanwhile, marriages that are already going strong can find additional ways to make their relationship even stronger. Here are some proven actions that can help improve your relationship.

Face your problems as a couple

1. Go beyond the blame game

The easy way out to any problem is to pin the blame on something or someone. It is not uncommon for some couples to put the blame on their partner when something goes wrong in the marriage. This is not a healthy habit, and it will only push you further away from each other. Both of you should go beyond the blame game when faced with problems.

Finding the solution to the problem is most of the time more important than criticizing who or what caused it. Instead of playing the blame game, both of you should figure out what to do next time so that problem would be avoided. It will save you from a lot of trouble and heartache.

2. Find solutions to your problems

Finding solutions to your problems is essential, especially if these are the types of problems that can affect your marriage. The best couples I know have created their own approach to solving problems, approaches that attack the problem in the most effective way possible without causing any unnecessary heartache.

Finding an approach that benefits both parties is proven to improve the health and longevity of marriages. It takes both time and familiarity with each other to find the best approach to combat your everyday problems.

3. Commit to solving your problems as a couple

This may sound cliché, but you are in it together in all aspects of your marriage. This includes solving the myriad of issues that you will face throughout your married life. It is important that both parties stay actively involved in both problem solving and decision making aspects.

A healthy marriage is wherein the couple works hand in hand in resolving issues both big and small. Also, both sides should be actively involved in all day-to-day tasks and decisions in the marriage, whether it is in the household or in business. Both of you should commit to solving your problems as a couple.

4. Look at the positive side of things

There are some situations wherein it is so difficult to look at the positive side of things. As time passes by, you see all the flaws and negative traits of your partner, and there are a lot of things that can go wrong. In spite of this, the better approach is still to focus on the positives. When you start thinking negative thoughts about your marriage or your partner, it is time to focus on the positives.

Instead of focusing on their flaws and wrongdoings, focus on the things that you love about them and the things they are doing right. Always be an encouraging presence and never forget to tell your spouse how much you appreciate them. Positivity goes a long way in keeping a marriage strong, so always keep the positivity up.

Have open communication with your partner

1. Define rules for conversations

Setting specific rules for conversations has proven to be convenient for most couples. Setting ground rules when you are together will give a structured approach to your daily talks. This will help ensure that your conversations remain productive and not breach the most basic lines of decency.

Examples of conversational rules include the following: no disrespectful language, pausing when emotions go out of hand, and no interrupting when the other person is talking. Different couples have different rules when it comes to conversations. It is up to both of you to set rules that you think would benefit your marriage best.

2. Make sure both sides feel respected

As we talked about in the chapters before, mutual respect is the foundation of all marriages. This should be evident even during your everyday conversations. It is important that respect never go away, even during times when conversations are veering towards more troublesome discussions. There are many ways to maintain respect when you are with your spouse. Pay full attention to your spouse when they are telling something to you. Avoid using provocative or disrespectful language. Never disrespect your partner or dismiss what they say just because you disagree with them.

3. Be the person you'll love to talk to

Perhaps the best way to open up communication lines with your partner is to become the person that they would love to talk to. When you become exactly the person that your partner loves to talk to, they can open up to you. There are many ways you can transform yourself into the ideal conversation partner.

Put a premium in listening to what the person says, and reserve talking to either push the tempo of the conversation or to help them further open up. Be open-minded and just listen to anything they have to say. Make yourself available for them and make them feel that you're there anytime they need someone to talk to.

4. Be genuine

Being real is one trait that is valued in all kinds of conversations. It helps that your spouse (as well as other people) knows what's in your mind, making it easier for them to trust you. When talking to your spouse, always be honest and tell them the truth. Let them know what you feel, what you think, and if you have any concern.

You should also practice being more comfortable in your own skin. When you are not self-confident or you're not proud of yourself, you end up pretending to be someone you are not. Lastly, never be afraid to admit your faults and failures.

Marriage basics to live by

1. Invest in improving your marriage

Many marriages become stagnant because the couple has stopped investing in their marriage and in each other. A marriage should be dynamic; it should adapt to the times and it should grow stronger in the face of mounting challenges. For a marriage to continuously grow, the couple should commit to its constant improvement.

It takes a lot of time and effort for it to be possible, and there would be times when conflicts can arise from it. However, it takes commitment from both sides to make all this possible. Discovering new things together, improving habits, and creating good memories are just some of the ways to take your marriage to the next level.

2. Value the little things

Every couple has a set of big goals for their marriage. These include being able to raise a successful family, have financial investments to last a lifetime, enjoy the bounties life has to offer, and stay happy as they advance in age. Regardless of what your goals and priorities are as a couple, it is important that you value the little things as well.

Be thankful for the simple things your spouse does

for you such as preparing meals or helping out with house chores. Always tell your spouse that you love him/her and that you appreciate their presence in your life. Celebrate each other's good times and be there for each other during the bad times. These little things may not seem grandiose, but they are the things that make a marriage worthwhile.

3. Learn to forgive

I got to break this to you: your partner is not going to be perfect. They are going to make mistakes that can sometimes break your heart, and they are going to have flaws that will make you cringe. In spite of these shortcomings, you got to learn how to forgive.

Forgiveness is such an important element for a marriage to work. A refusal to accept their flaws reflect a major attitude problem. Holding grudges will not just hold you back as a couple, but it will also prove a burden on your side. Lastly, not forgiving your spouse prevents your marriage from thriving. For a healthy marriage, learn to forgive your spouse as well as yourself.

4. Value each other's independence

Many married couples forget that even if they are already married, they are still individuals that are separate from their spouse. That said, one hallmark of healthy marriages is that they embrace the individuality of each other. There are many ways that a couple can embrace the individuality of each other.

You may have different interests, hobbies, beliefs, and careers, but you should still support each other in your respective pursuits. You should also refrain from trying to change the person according to your standards or how you want them to be. You should also respect each other's decisions.

Make the commitment

1. Never underestimate the demands of marriage

Getting married is not going to be easy. There are problems to be encountered along the way. A lot of people enter married life, thinking that it's going to be all roses. You will have to maintain the household, you will raise your family in the best way you can, you will have to handle all kinds of conflicts, and you will have to make some major choices.

It's not going to be an easy life once you get married. However, you got something that will help you overcome all that. It's none other than your spouse. Never underestimate the demands of marriage, but never undervalue the power of your marriage.

2. Make time for communication every day

As you progress with your marriage, there are a lot of things that will get in the way. There are responsibilities in both career and family. Sometimes, you will have to deal with factors such as time and distance. You will even get into each other's bad side every now and then. In spite of all this, you need to make time for communication every day.

One of the ways to keep your marriage alive is to communicate with each other. You can do it during work breaks, during shared meals, during the daily commute, or before you go to sleep.

3. Keep improving

One element that can cause the downfall of marriages is being stagnant. The couple can get bored, find that their relationship is not growing, and slowly become dissatisfied. Eventually, this opens the door for the decline of the marriage, which can eventually end up in the breakdown of the marriage.

The best antidote to this problem is to keep improving your marriage. A commitment to growing as a couple is the best defense to all forces that may tear you apart. At the same time, it will also be better if both husband and wife will stay committed to their personal growth. A commitment to constant improvement will benefit all marriages.

4. Keep the love alive

Love is the most fundamental ingredient in a marriage, the glue that holds everything together. When you marry, you and your partner make the vow to love each other until the last days of your lives. Marriage is a commitment that you made together, and ultimately it's a choice that you made out of your free will.

Essentially, love and marriage is a choice. Decide to love your spouse and commit to your marriage. There would be good and bad times. There would be difficulties. But as long as you are committed to getting the best out of your marriage, you and your spouse shall succeed in the long run.

Takeaway

- Improving your marriage is always possible, regardless of what the stage or state of your marriage.
- Fix your problems as a couple. Be the person that your spouse would love to share their problems with. Also, be genuine.
- There are some fundamentals in marriage that never go out of style. Always be committed to your marriage, value the little things, and value each other's individuality.
- Lastly, make the commitment to your marriage. Always communicate with each other, keep improving, and keep the love alive.

CONCLUSION

You have now reached the end of this book, and I would like to congratulate you for completing this book. I know that a lot of information and ideas have been shared in this book, but the fact that you have committed to completing this book means one thing: you are truly committed to making your marriage better. Congratulations once again, for this just might be the start of a new beginning for your marriage!

I hope you have learned a bunch of things from reading this book. Just to recap, here are some of the major things that you should take home from reading this book.

There are a lot of problems that you will encounter in your marriage. Furthermore, most of these problems are linked to lack of proper communication between you and your partner. This can be traced to a wide range of things, from the natural differences between male and female, to a lack of trust and commitment from you, your partner, or both.

The good thing is that there are many solutions available at your disposal. It all starts with improving your communication with your spouse. There are many ways to do this: make communication a habit, recognize the differences in your conversational style, put a premium on listening, and remember the basic rules and ethics of conversation.

Beyond this, you can improve the health of your conversations and your marriage in general by making some changes in the way you do things. Learning how to manage conflicts, having a positive outlook, and making your marriage a priority are some of the most important things all couples must remember.

Armed with this knowledge, the next step is to implement them in your everyday life! All the knowledge I've shared here would be useless if it's not put into action. For most couples, they may feel like my suggestions are a little too overwhelming. I've made the tips here as simple as possible to follow.

From there, all you have to do is to implement them in your everyday married life. You'll be surprised how these adjustments would improve your marriage in the long run. Whether you're going strong as a couple or you're having troubles, you will benefit from the advice I gave in this book.

I believe that all marriages deserve a chance to thrive. I also believe that every person deserves to have an awesome and fulfilling marriage. Now go ahead and create the best partnership ever, a partnership that brings joy and fulfillment for the rest of your days. I wish you good luck!

AUTHOR'S NOTE

Hi! Skyler here. I want to take a moment to personally thank you for reading my book. I hope that the information I provided in this book has been useful for you.

If you enjoyed reading the book, I would really appreciate it if you could write a short review. I'd love to read about your feedback as it really means a lot and keeps me going.

ABOUT THE AUTHOR

Skyler McCarty is a Self-Development Author and Communication Coach whose unwavering sense of perseverance and compassion have earned her the reputation as an advocate of positive change.

Throughout the past decade, she has cultivated extensive knowledge in the world's most powerful methods for personal and professional development. Currently, Skyler is working on a series of books that empower people to refine their interpersonal and intrapersonal skills, so they can pave the path to unshakable confidence.

Made in the USA
Middletown, DE
13 October 2024